"The first chapter of *Freedom from Wealth* is a must read for every wealth owner—shedding light on the difficult question of 'What is the wealth for?' The book also contains many useful tools that can free the wealth owner from the rigors of active wealth management by defining a structured process for financial oversight and governance. Readers will need to revisit these principles many times through the years."

—**Sara Hamilton**, author of *Family Legacy and Leadership*, founder and CEO of Family Office Exchange

"*Freedom from Wealth* is a welcome addition to the literature of wealth management. Among its many insights is one that is rarely offered by wealth advisers: the importance of placing philanthropy at the center of a wealth management strategy. Charles Lowenhaupt and Don Trone make a persuasive case for the potential of philanthropy to strengthen family bonds and to bring new meaning to the lives of wealthy people."

—**John R. Healy**, adjunct professor, Centre for Nonprofit Management, Trinity College Dublin; former president and CEO of the Atlantic Philanthropies

"Charles and Don offer practical, principled advice and guidance to wealth holders and their advisors in their comprehensive new book *Freedom from Wealth*. The chapters on the 'Importance of Strategy' are required reading for those seeking to advance beyond investments and harmonize all elements of wealth management."

—**Kathryn McCarthy**, advisor to Families and Family Offices; director, Rockefeller Trust Company N.A.

"When I sold [my] family's construction and property listed business in 2007, Charlie's perspective on wealth transfer and family succession proved invaluable. My luck in partnering with talented investors enabled me to build successful asset management enterprises, which has led to separate capital planning and education issues for my family and child. I benefitted greatly from Charlie's experience and guidance and am positive readers of the book will as well."

—**V-Nee Yeh,** Member of Executive Council, Hong Kong Government, cofounder and honorary chairman, Value Partners Limited; director, Hsin Chong International Holdings

"The relatively new advisory profession of coping with the benefits and problems of wealth will surely benefit the readers of this book. Charles Lowenhaupt is seriously well qualified to challenge conventional wisdom and tell us how to do it all better—and be happier as a result."

—**Robert McCuaig**, FRICS, cofounder, Advisory Board, Colliers International

"Very few advisors can deliver the longevity, the wisdom, the experience and the insights to assist families of wealth achieve consistent ethos in managing their assets. *Freedom from Wealth* is a must read for those who are serious in pursuing harmonization of the multiple facets of managing wealth for themselves or for their clients."

—**Francois M. de Visscher**, President of de Visscher & Co.; Greenwich, CT Board Member; BEKAERT NV, Belgium

FREEDOM

from

WEALTH

THE EXPERIENCE AND STRATEGIES TO HELP
PROTECT AND GROW PRIVATE WEALTH

CHARLES A. LOWENHAUPT
& DONALD B. TRONE

COFOUNDERS OF THE INSTITUTE FOR
WEALTH MANAGEMENT STANDARDS

New York Chicago San Francisco Lisbon London Madrid Mexico City
Milan New Delhi San Juan Seoul Singapore Sydney Toronto

Copyright © 2012 by Charles A. Lowenhaupt and Donald B. Trone. All rights reserved. Printed in the United States of America. Except as permitted under the United States Copyright Act of 1976, no part of this publication may be reproduced or distributed in any form or by any means, or stored in a database or retrieval system, without the prior written permission of the publisher.

2 3 4 5 6 7 8 9 10 11 12 13 14 15   QFR/QFR   1 9 8 7 6 5 4 3 2 1

ISBN   978-07-07-177763-6
MHID   0-07-177763-6

e-ISBN 978-0-07-177762-9
e-MHID   0-07-177762-8

This publication is designed to provide accurate and authoritative information in regard to the subject matter covered. It is sold with the understanding that neither the author nor the publisher is engaged in rendering legal, accounting, securities trading, or other professional services. If legal advice or other expert assistance is required, the services of a competent professional person should be sought.
> —*From a Declaration of Principles Jointly Adopted by a Committee of the American Bar Association and a Committee of Publishers and Associations*

Library of Congress Cataloging-in-Publication Data

Lowenhaupt, Charles.
    Freedom from wealth : the experience and strategies to help protect and grow private wealth / by Charles Lowenhaupt and Don Trone.
      p.   cm.
    ISBN-13: 978-0-07-177763-6 (hardback : acid-free paper)
    ISBN-10: 0-07-177763-6 (hardback : acid-free paper)
    1. Wealth.   2. Wealth—Management.   3. Finance, Personal.   I. Trone, Donald B.   II. Title.

    HB251.L69   2011
    332.024′01—dc23   2011019479

Interior design by Think Book Works

McGraw-Hill books are available at special quantity discounts to use as premiums and sales promotions or for use in corporate training programs. To contact a representative, please e-mail us at bulksales@mcgraw-hill.com.

This book is printed on acid-free paper.

Contents

Acknowledgments   **vii**

Overview   **ix**

The Principles of Wealth Management   **xiii**

PART 1 Reflections on Wealth Management

1   What Is the Wealth For?   **3**

2   Freedom from Wealth   **11**

3   Individuality and Wealth   **17**

4   The Importance of Comfort   **27**

5   The Importance of Strategy: Overview   **33**

6   The Importance of Strategy: Philanthropy   **37**

7   The Importance of Strategy: Investment Policies   **43**

8   The Importance of Strategy: Capitalization   **69**

9   The Importance of Strategy: Governance   **75**

10   The Importance of Strategy: Family Legacy and Values   **95**

11   The Importance of Strategy: Next Generation Education   **99**

12   The Role of Wealth Management Standards   **103**

13   The Transition from Reflections to Implementation   **111**

PART 2 Principles of Wealth Management for Private Wealth Holders
and Related Parties

14 The Standards Director 117

15 The Ethos Decision-Making Framework 121

16 Step 1: Analyze 133

17 Step 2: Strategize 145

18 Step 3: Formalize 163

19 Step 4: Implement 177

20 Step 5: Monitor 195

21 Assessment Procedures 213

Appendix Sample Private Wealth Policy Statement (PWPS) 221

Index 235

Acknowledgments

SOUND PROCESS CAN BEST BE BUILT WITH OPPORTUNITIES TO STUDY models and consult with experts. Wisdom requires wise heads thinking together and providing inspiration and guidance. There are those without whose guidance and wisdom this book could not have been written. Some of those include:

- Clients and colleagues from around the world whose experiences and insights infuse all of our writing
- Organizations with which we have been fortunate to associate and where colleagues have given us the freedom to enhance and pursue our thinking, including the Foundation for Fiduciary Studies, Lowenhaupt Global Advisors, Lowenhaupt and Chasnoff, the Institute for Wealth Management Standards, and the Institute for Private Investors
- Those who have contributed directly and indirectly to the content of this volume, including members of the Lowenhaupt Global Advisors Global Council, Greg Berardi of Blue Marlin Partners, Daniel Crewe of Profile Books, Alexander Haverstick of Boxwood Strategic Advisors, HR Chally, and Eric L. Herzog, Ph.D.
- Those whose support has been fundamental to the Institute for Wealth Management and the standards initiative: John Pettifor of Campden Conferences, Stephen Fern of G9, Dr. Tis Prager of Prager Dreifuss, and Family Office Exchange
- Our wives and families, whose support and patience have made our work possible
- Henry Lowenhaupt, whose guidance, wisdom, and humanity underlie so many of the reflections in this book

Overview

HOW DO YOU MANAGE YOUR WEALTH WISELY? WHAT IS THE UNDER-standing and what are the tools that you need to make your wealth accomplish what it should accomplish? Those are the questions we attempt to resolve in this volume. The answers will allow wealth holders to work effectively with their family offices, their trusted advisors, and their financial services professionals. We also provide family offices, advisors, and wealth managers the tools and processes needed to serve their clients.

Wisdom in wealth management comes from:

+ Experience, which gives understanding
+ Strategic thinking to see how each decision furthers a purpose
+ Caring about the people you want to benefit and the people who will help you, all with a foundation of humanistic understanding
+ Respect for discipline and process

Creativity can help us use wisdom but itself is not wisdom. Shrewdness, cleverness, or "brilliance" do not necessarily lead to wisdom except where they lead to adherence to wisdom-infused process.

The understanding of wisdom becomes important when we consider private wealth management. As is often said, institutional wealth management—managing endowments, pensions, superannuation, government and corporate funds—is different from private wealth management. Much institutional wealth management is governed by rules and regulations, whether fiduciary rules, statutes, and regulations or standards set by committee, and most drafters of those rules believe they are wise. Private wealth, whether run by an individual, a financial services company, or a family office, has had no generally accepted rules guiding its management. Providers may be regulated, but the wealth holders themselves are not.

Most people are amateurs at managing their own wealth. In good times, amateurs do well by picking stocks, investment advisors, strategies, and programs using foundational instincts such as trust, appearance, and shrewdness. In bad times, those instinctual guides are as likely to hurt as help. We saw this in 2007 and 2008 when giants in the financial services industry, such as Bear Stearns, Lehman, AIG, and others, proved unreliable and unsustainable.

So by 2008, the question became pressing: How should private wealth holders infuse wisdom into their management of private wealth? That requires looking at wealth management broadly to include all elements of how a person relates to his or her wealth. How to manage wealth cannot be considered without considering what the wealth is for. What does the person want the wealth to accomplish?

Infusing wisdom into one's wealth management requires analysis. All of the talk of trust and integrity surrounding Bernie Madoff, Stanford Financial, Lehman, AIG, and the other horrors of the year suggested that wisdom lay in finding true integrity and grounds for trust; and the common buzz was that if one found trustworthy advisors, wealth could be well managed. There was a renewed focus on shrewdness and cleverness—the good and bad of it.

Informed by the views of wise wealth holders and experienced advisors to private wealth around the world, we concluded that wisdom required establishing certain fundamental principles for private wealth management. Those principles would not be aspirational, they would not be "best practices," and they would not be complex. They would be recognized by all as principles that made sense but could be fitted wealth holder by wealth holder to his or her situation. Those principles would be universal but flexible. They would be grounded in experience. They would be like fiduciary guidelines, capable of interpretation but also capable of evaluation.

Overall, the principles would be intended to cover all areas of a person's relationship to his or her wealth to allow the development and harmonization of strategies to accomplish specific, well-defined purposes. They would also serve as a foundation for an adaptable system of implementation and monitoring.

Those became Principles of Wealth Management for Private Wealth Holders and Related Parties. Originally promulgated by Lowenhaupt Global Advisors' Global Council, those Principles are now being used by the Institute for Wealth Management Standards, a not-for-profit enterprise, to develop Standards for Private Wealth Management. Those Standards, principles-based and therefore adaptable to each individual, set out the framework for operation under the Principles. They provide for a Standards Director for each wealth holder or family, and they assume that a Standards Director will be a kind of chief operating officer to make the Standards work.

This volume is an attempt to set out the experience, the strategic thinking, the humanistic understanding, and the respect for process that inform the Principles of Wealth Management for Private Wealth Holders and Related Parties. We start by sharing those elements that have led to wealth management wisdom and then bring that theoretical knowledge into practical application through analysis of how to select a Standards Director and how that person can implement the Principles using the Standards that have been designed by the institute.

Charles Lowenhaupt has worked with private clients in the company founded by his grandfather more than 100 years ago. He has met with scores of wealth holders, family office experts, and financial services providers over his 40 years in the industry. His learning from clients and other wealth holders is the basis for the wisdom underlying the Principles. He and Donald Trone and the Lowenhaupt Global Advisors Global Council developed the Principles themselves as well as the concept that the Principles should be the basis for the Standards. Working under the auspices of the Institute for Wealth Management Standards, Donald Trone has drafted the first generation of the Standards.

This book is divided into two sections. Part 1, "Reflections on Wealth Management," was written primarily by Charles Lowenhaupt and sets out the foundations of the wisdom and process embodied in the Principles. Part 2, "Principles of Wealth Management for Private

Wealth Holders and Related Parties," is authored primarily by Donald Trone and is an explanation of how a Standards Director can use the Standards to bring wisdom and process to a wealth holder. Together we hope to give wealth holders and Standards Directors the understanding and tools they need to manage wealth to accomplish its purposes.

The Principles of Wealth Management

WISDOM AND PROCESS ARE THE FOUNDATIONS OF SOUND WEALTH management. Strategies must be developed that allow the harmonization of all elements of wealth management—from investments to philanthropy to governance to education and well beyond.

The building blocks of wisdom are principles:

+ They are principles—not rules.
+ They are fundamental—not best practices.
+ They are ideals—not absolutes.
+ They are simple—not intended to be complex or controversial.

The Principles of Wealth Management for Private Wealth Holders and Related Parties are intended to be inclusive of and provide guidelines for all elements of a person's relationship to his or her wealth. They allow the harmonization of services and strategies. As principles, they can be selected, modified, and adjusted individual by individual and family by family. But first and foremost, they are the guiding principles that lay down the foundation of process-driven wealth management.

The Principles of Wealth Management were developed by Lowenhaupt Global Advisors and adopted by its Global Council in January 2009.

PRINCIPLES OF WEALTH MANAGEMENT
FOR PRIVATE WEALTH HOLDERS

1. The wealth holder, the trustees of a trust, or the directors of a foundation shall articulate purposes, goals, objectives, expectations, and risk tolerance with respect to the wealth and shall be ultimately responsible for maintaining the currency of that articulation.

2. With respect to a family office, a trust, or a foundation, the governance structure together with various governance roles and responsibilities shall be clearly set forth and shall include provision for the communication of those roles and responsibilities and assurance that they are understood and accepted.

3. Any trust or foundation and any trustee or director shall adhere to best fiduciary practices, and there shall be an established process for monitoring the discharge of fiduciary duties by the trust, foundation, trustee, or director.

4. Succession shall be set out where possible and shall be considered. For the wealth holder provisions shall be in existence for disposition of assets and management of affairs from and after death or in the event of incapacity. For the family office, trust, or foundation, provision shall be made for succession of governance and management.

5. Each investment portfolio shall be diversified as completely as is practical. There should be diversification of asset classes, investment managers, investment style, currencies, banking and brokerage exposure, and geopolitical risks.

6. Every portfolio shall have an investment policy statement, and every manager shall have a clearly articulated mandate; the investment policy statement and mandate shall be monitored.

7. Any investment portfolio shall be designed taking into account the assets, objectives, needs, and character of the owner and/or beneficiary and should be monitored with those in mind; a foundation shall have a process to determine whether the investment program reflects the values of its mission and its philanthropic grant program.

8. There shall be a clear, disciplined, and objective process for selecting, monitoring, removing, and replacing investment

managers, custodians, banks, and trade execution, accounting, and other professionals.

9. Any investment manager or specific fund to be used shall
   have a strategy and style that can be easily understood and
   explained to others by the wealth holder or by one of the
   trustees, directors, or staff members of the trust, foundation,
   or family office. If no one other than the investment manager
   or the fund representative is able to explain the strategy and
   style, the manager or fund shall not be used.

10. Special scrutiny and limitations should be applied to any
    investment manager who does not provide complete trans-
    parency or whose portfolio is not liquid; such investments are
    not prohibited but should be limited in proportion to total
    portfolio investments.

11. Custody of assets, accounting for assets, and investment man-
    agement services shall each be performed independently and
    separately.

12. There shall be an established process for managing and moni-
    toring internal and external resources.

13. There shall be full transparency of fees and expenses.

14. Compensation and fees paid to staff, directors, and governors
    of family offices, foundations, or boards shall not be calculated
    on the basis of investment return of shorter duration than five
    years. Any salary, bonus, or fee must be fully disclosed as to
    its amount and its calculation. Any direct or indirect payment
    to or for staff or governors other than a payment-designated
    salary, bonus, or fee (or similar designation) is prohibited.

15. Self-dealing by staff, trustees, or directors of any family office,
    trust, or foundation is strictly prohibited. Investment portfo-
    lios of those parties shall be subject to strict disclosure rules
    that assure compliance with the prohibition against self-
    dealing. Any grant or payment to any agency or company in
    which such a party has any interest whatsoever should clearly
    reflect that interest in the deliberation relating to that grant or
    payment.

PART 1

Reflections on Wealth Management

1

What Is the Wealth For?

Wealth is the slave of a wise man. The master of a fool.
—SENECA (5 B.C.–A.D. 65)

WHEN IT COMES TO SIGNIFICANT FAMILY WEALTH, THE STARTING question is always, what is the wealth for? That is an easy question to ask and a very difficult question to answer.

It is much easier to say what the wealth is not for, including the following:

+ I don't want it used for taxes.
+ I don't want it squandered.
+ I don't want my spouse to take it in a divorce.
+ I don't believe in charity, so it is not for charity.
+ I don't want my children to have it too young.
+ I don't want the lawyers using it all up in fees.

Any of these statements may be reasonable. None answers the question what the wealth is for.

Wealth is always to support the wealth holder with reasonable necessities of life—food, clothing, housing, and some luxuries. And for most people, wealth is for the education of children and possibly grandchildren. But there are amounts of wealth beyond those reasonably needed for living. If wealth is for something other than extravagant consumption, the question always remains, what is the wealth for? Surprisingly, it is a question that rarely gets asked, nor is it revisited in the few cases it is initially asked.

I have spoken at wealth conferences around the world. Whether in Mumbai, London, or New York, members of the audience come up to me afterward and say that the question has never been posed to them before. Is it a valid question in the first place, I ask? It is, they answer. But it is a dangerous question for a service provider to ask because if accomplishing the wealth's purposes does not require products being sold, there can be no sale and no profit from the prospect.

The story of a 95-year-old man who came to see me many years ago illustrates this point. This gentleman was a Holocaust survivor, unmarried, and without children. He was planning his estate and I asked him about his assets. He had all of his wealth, more than $1 million (then a great amount) in treasury bills in custody at the Federal Reserve. I asked him whether he should consider asset allocation, inflation, efficient frontiers, and so on. He answered, "This money is to take care of me during my lifetime. It serves its purpose best in cash equivalents, and at my age I have no concern about inflation." He knew what the wealth was for and had absolutely no need for financial services advisors much less any of their products.

An accidental wealth holder who came into my office several years ago had invested in a friend's business 30 years earlier and came to own stock worth $800 million. He explained that he came to see me because he wanted to save taxes. "That is fine," I said. "We can do that and have been doing it for 95 years. But you are telling me what you do not want your wealth used for—taxes. What *do* you want your wealth used for?" He asked me what I meant, and I said, "What are the purposes you want to accomplish with your wealth?" His reply was one that I had not heard before: "Well, what are my choices?" I laughed at first and then told him the question was actually an excellent one. What are the choices?

In fact, the choices are not so many if we are talking about substantial wealth that is to be multigenerational. Broadly speaking, there are only two choices, though there may be gradations between them.

First, wealth can be for freedom and functionality. The idea is that the functional person with freedom can be whatever he or she wants to be. Second, wealth can be for control, so that a person's children and grandchildren can live without concern or involvement with his or her wealth.

When I set out those choices—freedom and functionality, or control—the accidental wealth holder said he could tell which I endorsed. The benefits of freedom and functionality were clear in the very words I used. But the accidental wealth holder believed that control was a negative concept. I replied that I endorsed neither and was in fact neutral. If instead of "control" I had said "protection," my perspective may seem less biased. An analogy helps clarify the point. A Benedictine monk, living in a very controlled monastery, with access to neither money nor control over the way affairs are handled, has complete intellectual freedom. He is liberated of any concern about paying mortgages, investing monastic funds, or even where and what he will have for dinner.

So either choice can provide self-actualization if handled correctly. However, risk is implicit in both. To make wealth deliver freedom and functionality without protection requires that the children or grandchildren be allowed to lose the money. In essence, they have to be free to fail. When a parent teaches a child to ride a bike, the parent must be prepared for the risk that the child will fall. I told the accidental wealth holder that he had to be prepared for his children or grandchildren to lose the money, to return to shirtsleeves, if he was to choose the course of freedom and functionality.

The risk of choosing control or protection lies in the danger that one's children may have believed the wealth was for freedom and functionality and would be hurt to learn it was not. The purpose of the wealth—protection—must be shared early with the entire family. I told the accidental wealth holder about a family my father and I had worked with many years earlier. The patriarch had decided he would protect his heirs forever; his purpose for his wealth was control. We called the entire family, three sons in their midtwenties, together and told them that. Each moved on with his life—one became a doctor, one became a lawyer, and one became the "family wealth steward," that is, the person who took care of the family's finances and also a major philanthropist. Today, they are all over 40 and happily engaged in life and not bothered by the fact that their assets are all in trust and under control. In this case, letting the children know that the patriarch would design "protection" through control allowed each to move on with life.

In fact, whether the wealth is for freedom and functionality or simply control, it can give future generations the capacity to live life to its fullest. Indeed, whatever wealth is for, each wealth holder should be free to lead a fully self-actualized life—to be all he or she can be. There can be no reasonable debate about that. As the accidental wealth holder saw in my example, the patriarch who explained that the wealth would be controlled gave his sons the liberation from feelings of resentment or anticipation that they needed to get on with their lives.

It is critical, then, to start by deciding and articulating what the wealth is for. The answer can change, but until an answer is clear, any wealth management program will be a multitude of trees and not a forest. Once the answer is obvious, a management program can be designed to accomplish the purposes. Wealth holders and their advisors can utilize tactics, strategies, and opportunities and set goals. Crises, taxes, investment losses, and other hurtful events are merely impediments to accomplishing the purposes of the wealth and are not in and of themselves damaging.

How does one go about trying to answer the question, what is my wealth for? One must start by relying on wisdom and implementing sound process. Wisdom comes from experiencing life, from reading and studying the humanities (Shakespeare is quite helpful—think *King Lear* or *Merchant of Venice*). Wisdom can also come by relying on a trusted advisor who asks questions objectively and talks through the consequences of any answer. One can more easily harness and apply all this wisdom through process. Find some method of decision making that gives structure to your deliberation.

It would be much easier if there were in fact more choices. Yet, reasonable consideration removes many of the choices people look to as easy. All of the "what it is not for" answers are not choices. Creation and preservation are not choices. Wealth is created or preserved so that it can meet its purposes; however, creation and preservation are not the purposes in and of themselves.

Consider several examples of sophisticated wealth holders who answered the question with clarity.

One is a woman I knew when she was very old. She came from a Texas family of great oil wealth and married a Connecticut Yankee, a hardworking graduate of Yale. Before her wedding she told her fiancé: "My daddy handles my money and I don't worry my pretty little head about it." She left her money in a trust managed in Texas, while together she and her husband built a life and family and he built a career. "We used my money for incidentals—a vacation now and then, college for the children, some improvements to our house." Her wealth was for "icing on the cake" but would not become part of their relationship or their marriage. She said to me: "Life is full of ups and downs, happiness and sadness, successes and losses, good health and bad. Why complicate relationships and life with money management?" Her wealth was well positioned; she turned her attention to her husband and the family. The wealth was for no more than allowing them to live a full life.

Another is a wealth inheritor who was the son of a Holocaust survivor. His father had lost his first wife and children in a concentration camp and had married the wealth inheritor's mother when they met in the camp shortly before liberation. His parents moved to Germany after their marriage because his father learned that he could recover his business if he remained in Germany for a period of time. The wealth inheritor grew up as a Jew in postwar Germany for 10 years, while the father pushed his case for the return of his business. When the business was finally returned, the father moved the family to Switzerland. What was the wealth for? It was to ensure that the wealth inheritor and his descendants always had sufficient funds and associations to move wherever and whenever they had to move to stay free and alive. Residences in Switzerland and a number of other jurisdictions, bank accounts around the world, and business associates and investments in Europe, the United States, Asia, and South America were in place so that he and his children could flee and settle anywhere. The wealth was for freedom of movement.

Others conclude that the wealth is only indirectly for family and use it to improve their world through philanthropy. A wealth inheritor told me: "My wealth is for me to spend and for me to serve on charitable boards. If anything is left for my children, so be it."

A wealth creator in Asia told me, "My wealth is to build a dynasty." That rarely works because although the creator may have a vision, it may be a difficult vision for the children to share. *Dynastic* here means simply having lots of money for many generations; the money is there to be used for a purpose, but possessing it is not a purpose in and of itself.

"What is the wealth for?" appears to be a simple question, yet answering it often is not simple. However, once the answer is clear, developing the details of wealth management becomes easy by applying wisdom and process.

Asking the question is central to building wealth management programs. It may even be fundamental if one intends to harmonize money and life. Nevertheless, there are those for whom the answer is instinctual and the question answered even without asking it.

I was a young lawyer and my senior partner, my father, asked me to meet with a longtime client, often called "the indomitable no man," about his estate planning. In those days, this man seemed awfully old—70—and awfully rich—$10 million at least. He had been widowed and had married what we would now call a "trophy wife." He had two children and several grandchildren.

Our morning meeting started with my review of the estate tax laws as they existed, an analysis of his trusts and will, and some talk of estate preservation. He did not seem terribly interested; indeed he seemed somewhat tired. As I moved into detail, I noticed that he started to nod and doze, though I could awaken him with an occasional reference to his death and probate administration.

An hour or so into our meeting, I was just starting to cover the most significant aspects and opportunities that would be available to him with careful and intricate planning when he looked at his watch and stood up. "Thank you very much but my wife is waiting for me. We are playing golf this morning," he said. I asked him when we could reconvene and he looked puzzled. He thought we had finished our conversation.

Convinced that I could turn the corner on his attention I said, "What about providing for your grandchildren and their children, what about the opportunities to have your wealth skip generations, what about the inter vivos gifts you can make without substantial transfer taxes? Think of all you can do now."

He looked at me intently. For the first time that morning, he showed some passion. "Young man, I have a life to lead and a wife to spend time with. Why should I worry about such things as trusts, estate taxes, and future generations? I see no reason to worry about my grandchildren and my great-grandchildren. What has posterity ever done for me?"

I had assumed that "what the wealth was for" had something to do with future generations, with providing wealth for self-actualization and liberation. That was erroneous. He was not the least bit interested in his children, grandchildren, and all future generations. He was simply living his life and having a real good time. For him that was what the wealth was for and that was enough.

2

Freedom from Wealth

IN HIS THEORIES ON HUMAN MOTIVATION, THE PSYCHOLOGIST Abraham H. Maslow addressed the concept of self-actualization:

> Even if all these [fundamental] needs are satisfied, we may still often (if not always) expect that a new discontent and restlessness will soon develop, unless the individual is doing what he is fitted for. A musician must make music, an artist must paint, a poet must write, if he is to be ultimately happy. What a man *can* be, he *must* be. This need we may call self-actualization.
>
> —A. H. Maslow, "A Theory of Human Motivation"

Every person should strive to live life to the fullest, to become all that he or she is capable of becoming, to be self-actualized. If there is any goal for any wealth holder, it should be freedom from wealth. Yet, we live in a world where an industry has been built on the proposition that inherited wealth must be preserved and that preserving it requires substantial commitment and attention on the part of the wealth inheritor. Few talk about using wealth to create freedom from its burdens.

Consider the story of the patriarch who recognized that the wealth was for control and shared that with his sons. Two of the boys went off to lead full lives as lawyer and doctor, while one became the "wealth steward." The patriarch intended the money to provide control and not directly to encourage freedom and functionality. Yet through sharing the purpose, the father effectively liberated two of his sons from the burden of managing the wealth and of letting it control their lives. Those two sons got freedom from wealth. The third son became a wealth steward and spent his life taking care of the family money.

The wealth management industry unnecessarily reinforces the notion that managing significant wealth often carries burdensome responsibility. I was conducting a session with an elderly client who had started with nothing and built a fortune over his lifetime. I was introducing him to the concept of a family office, and we were considering his grandson as steward of the family wealth. The grandson would be responsible for perpetual trusts to be created for future generations. I was using the language that the wealth management industry uses for best practices. I talked about stewardship, preservation of wealth and capital, encouraging family values, developing trusts, partnerships, and other vehicles to be governed in accordance with fiduciary standards by his children, grandchildren, and beyond.

I stopped to ask the old man how he would have reacted to this conversation when he was 50 years younger and just dreaming of creating wealth. What would he then have said to my grandfather (whom he called "Uncle Abe") if my grandfather had told him he would have hundreds of millions of dollars and would be using words like *responsibility, stewardship, governance structures,* and *fiduciary?*

The old man laughed: "I would have said 'Uncle Abe, you are nuts. Those are not the words I would be using about my wealth. I would have used the words *freedom, independence,* and *living life to its fullest.*'"

Another story illustrates the same point about the burdens of wealth, but through the eyes of the wealth inheritor. I was scheduled to give a talk on freedom from wealth at a family wealth conference. Over lunch before my session, I sat next to a woman who introduced herself as an artist. She was highly accomplished; she had won prizes and taught at a prestigious university. I was impressed by her credentials. She was also from a very wealthy family. I asked her why she was at the conference, and she told me it was to learn about hedge funds.

"Really, are you interested in hedge funds?" I asked.

"No, but the family office has said we must decide whether to invest in hedge funds, and I am on the committee to decide. I am here to learn about hedge funds."

She asked what I was doing there. When I told her I was speaking about freedom from wealth and explained what that meant, she said she was interested. I invited her to my session but she said she could not make it because she would then be attending the session about hedge funds. I had begun my talk on freedom from wealth when, within five minutes, she walked in the back door and sat down. After I finished my presentation, I asked her what happened.

She said, "I sat through the first few minutes of that hedge fund session terribly bored. The refrain 'freedom from wealth' played in my mind until I decided to hell with hedge funds. I am an artist. I can hire people to decide whether and how to invest in hedge funds."

I saw my artist several months later. She said that her decision to leave that hedge fund session changed the way she was willing to view her wealth and her life. She would look for freedom to be an artist.

Everywhere, we see the same yearning for the capacity to live one's life fully and freely. The Holocaust survivor from Chapter 1 built his wealth around freedom of movement—houses in jurisdictions around the world. A young Australian wealth inheritor said he does not like sitting around a table reading investment reports and "contemplating the navel of my wealth. I want to live life—I have passions I am pursuing in active business." A 30-year-old U.S. wealth creator moving into a new venture said of his wealth management advisors, "They are wonderful. I know they are worrying about my portfolio and making sure it is working for me. That leaves me free to build my new business, to do what I want to do." Or consider the young Malaysian wealth creator who said, "I am building businesses one after the other; but when I sell one, I throw the proceeds over my shoulder and no one catches them to manage them. I don't care because I am having too much fun creating new businesses to worry about the proceeds of the old ones."

How many inheritors find wealth as their only career? They are spending more and more time "working" on their wealth, managing managers, evaluating performance, and mastering the pros and cons of new investment techniques. There are volumes of research and hours of educational programs devoted to the intricacies of investing, tax strategies, and estate planning, all pointing toward the need for multiple levels of expertise. Even the process of growing up rich has become so intricate that we have expert consultants to advise parents how to parent with wealth.

Pity the poor family member who becomes the "family wealth steward." These are not the wealth creators but instead are family members on whom has fallen the mantle of "fiduciary responsibility" to maintain and preserve the wealth. They are the high priests of the sanctity of family wealth, the silent butlers serving the family over generations. Their mantra is fiduciary responsibility, and their goal is to beat the "shirtsleeves to shirtsleeves" cycle. They are central actors in a cast designed by the wealth management industry, supporting actors to the banks, trust companies, lawyers, money managers, family wealth consultants, family office executives, and so on. They are family members for whom family wealth has become a full-time occupation.

The family member who is the family wealth steward is hardly ever happy in that role. When portfolios go up, they go up with the market. When they go down, it is the steward's fault. There is a U.S. family of four children. One son is a doctor, one son is a diplomat, one daughter is a professor of archaeology, and one son is the family wealth steward. The steward was enjoying his life in the years of up markets and wild successes. But when the market went down or when 5 percent return became a hurdle to try to meet, his enjoyment paled compared to the diplomat negotiating treaties, the doctor working on genome sequence, and the daughter excavating ruins in Italy.

Parents today raise their children to believe they can be whatever they want to be. Families in China and India are raising their first generation of wealth consumers. Children from Shanghai and Bombay are being educated with children from Los Angeles and Paris. A child from Jakarta goes to college in Melbourne. The child of a South African refugee may marry the grandchild of a Bolshevik bureaucrat. The human value all of them share is the vision of liberty and freedom. Americans, Chinese, Indians, Australians, Africans, and Europeans all see in that vision unlimited opportunities. If those unlimited opportunities shine in the eyes of the child out of *Slumdog Millionaire*, why should the child of wealth wear blinders? No, freedom is for everyone!

What is wealth for? We find universal and global agreement that it is not to cause unhappiness. It is not to create fiduciary burdens. It is not to enslave in governance structures. It is not to be weighed down with responsibilities. Freedom from wealth, getting on with life, self-actualization—all have to be possible in whatever design is created to make the wealth do what it is for. Gaining freedom from the burdens of wealth requires wisdom and process—wisdom to allow perspective and process to allow delegation of the minutiae. Together those can provide comfort to lead life free of the burdens of wealth.

Wisdom dictates that when a wealth holder is delegating the details of wealth management, he or she should ensure that processes are articulated and assessable. Without sound process one may delegate to Bernie Madoff or Lehman or others who betray trust. Principles and standards provide the sound management process. Better process and more wisdom can provide comfort to lead life free of the burdens of wealth.

Individuality and Wealth

Get to know two things about a man—how he earns his money and how he spends it—and you have the clue to his character, for you have a searchlight that shows up the innermost recesses of his soul. You know all you need to know about his standards, his motives, his driving desires, and his real religion.

—ROBERT J. MCCRACKEN

THE WEALTH INDUSTRY OFTEN TALKS ABOUT SOMETHING CALLED "family wealth management." Whether that means family office services offered by a bank, a multifamily office, family wealth conferences, books about family wealth, or experts in family wealth, the focus seems to be on *family*. Indeed, "family office" combines the feel-good word *family* and the business word *office* to give the implicit message that *family* is a unit, an almost monolithic entity. Services and products can then be bundled in the office or the service provider, and efficiencies of scale follow for the family or the provider.

It is time to step back and recognize that a family is not monolithic but is instead made up of individuals with different lives, different spouses, different children, different challenges and aspirations, possibly different jurisdictions, and possibly different cultures. And each of those individuals may have his or her own answer to the question, what is the wealth for?

If family members are treated as mere building blocks of a monolithic entity, individuality is suppressed and the family eclipses any personal vision of self. A patriarch or matriarch views the concept of immediate family as his or her children and all of their descendants; one of the children may view immediate family as himself or herself and his or her descendants. In other words, each may define *family* differently. A wealth creator often thinks in terms of keeping the family together rather than giving offspring and future generations the latitude to use the wealth to lead lives of their own making. The wealth, then, is not the dynamic driver of individual progress but rather a constraining and defining force that often leads to unhappiness.

Families around the world frequently wrestle with the challenge of treating family as other than a monolithic entity. Sometimes, the family monolith is seen as cultural; sometimes it is seen as inherent in wealth; and sometimes it is seen as efficient. However it is seen, "family" as the ultimate entity to be serviced and considered almost always results in unhappiness as it enslaves the individual.

Many years ago as China saw the glimmer of private wealth on its horizons, a Shanghai scholar told me that one of the differences I would encounter working with Chinese families ("This is quite unique," he said) is that the wealth is not seen as owned by individuals. Instead, it is seen as owned by the family. "That would be unusual," I said. But first we must analyze *ownership*. It consists of two elements: the control of the assets and the economic interest in the assets. In common law jurisdictions, we sometimes say that a trustee has *legal* title, shorthand for apparent control, and the beneficiary has *equitable* interest, shorthand for economic benefit.

Broken into these elements of ownership, how can a family—a group of people—own property? They cannot each have full economic benefit of the entire amount—division must take place on some level. And they cannot each have full control of the entire amount. At the very least, they must somehow share control and benefit.

To illustrate the point, it's useful to consider the ownership of a publicly held company—say, Microsoft. We can say that Microsoft owns various assets, but Microsoft exists only formally and structurally. Its shareholders ultimately have the economic benefit of those assets, and its shareholders ultimately are individuals, whether through trusts, pension plans, or otherwise. The control of the assets is exercised by Microsoft. But Microsoft is ultimately controlled by legal and regulatory constructs and, more important, shareholders exercising that control generally through participatory vote.

In fact, I have heard many people describe their wealth as "family wealth" just as my Chinese scholar friend described it. But I have never found the family that can ultimately treat the family as the absolute owner. In my work with Chinese families and many others, I find that the wealth creator more often than not wants to control the wealth. I know of one family where the patriarch told his five children that he was ready for them to take on all attributes of ownership, and he meant it. Yet it took his children five years of struggle with role and respect to grow into a willingness to take on attributes of ownership.

Another Chinese wealth inheritor, a man with young children and a sister, after the death of his father told me the story of his family wealth. His great-grandfather and his great-grandfather's brother had fought over the family business at the end of the nineteenth century. His great-grandfather had won the business after a rancorous battle, leaving the two brothers estranged. Then his grandfather had a similar fight with his own brother and won the business. His father had fought over the business with his aunt, and his father had won that battle. "When will you and your sister start fighting?" I asked. He looked puzzled and asked why I would think they might fight. With so many divisions, how could one call that a family "owning" the family wealth?

In New Delhi, a friend of mine—a trusted advisor to a number of wealthy families—explained that Indian wealth has a tradition of dividing the business at each generation, often rancorously. He believed businesses prosper that way and cited the Ambani family as an example. After the two brothers separated, they were worth more than they would have been together, he thought. Primogeniture managed to concentrate wealth in England for many years and incidentally allowed the settlement of colonies by the younger brothers who never inherited the real estate. In this case, "family wealth" meant ownership by the oldest son.

In Europe, a wealth creator had transferred some of the company stock to his two children. A subsequent liquidity event created great wealth for himself and his children. The wealth creator called his children together and said: "This is not my wealth or your wealth; this is family wealth to be shared." The speech he gave was inspirational according to his children and ended with his saying that all the wealth should be recombined to be held and managed together with his wealth for the benefit of the children and himself. The children, then both in college, agreed immediately. I met this family 10 years later. The patriarch was still saying the wealth was "family wealth," but he was spending without restraint and investing and managing without restraint. Processes his children tried to set up for investment discipline, for cash management and budgeting, he endorsed heartily, but then considered them applicable to the children and not to himself. The patriarch was squandering all of the wealth, both his and his children's. He confided to me that what he meant by "family" was that after his death it would be all theirs, unless he decided to give it to his new girlfriend, who might become his wife.

The attitude of that European wealth creator is not unique. In fact, it should be his wealth—he created it. There is no need for him to think in terms of "stewardship" except to the extent he had already given the wealth away. Indeed, some of the most complex and arcane structuring in the estate planning world is designed to try to keep control and access in the hands of the "donor." The person making gifts to children, grandchildren, family, and charity does so using complex trusts and partnerships to preserve his or her control without crossing the lines of tax regulation or standards required for protection against creditors. Wealth creators, indeed wealth owners, do not like to cede control or access to the wealth. For the wealth creator, the monolithic family is usually everyone but himself or herself. "Family wealth" often means control by the wealth creator.

The concept of family wealth held by that wealth creator ends up taking on a life of its own. The wealth creator has a family, possibly some children and a spouse. While the children are young, he or she can think of the nuclear family, living together, growing together, and completely bundled at least into the teen years. But the wealth creator's way of thinking does not easily disappear so that when the family is sitting around the "board table," they remember sitting around the dining room table when the youngest child was two. Maturity and process do not intuitively fit. The systems and thinking become fossilized into structures, family offices, and family dynamics even after the wealth creator at the center of those systems and thinking has died—a rock-hard shell of governance, mineralized around an empty center.

Most family wealth programs and family offices fail because they do not recognize the individual. The fossil, the mineralized structure of multigenerational family wealth management, is without the central personality, the soft tissue, of the wealth creator and does not take into account the individual's need to self-actualize. Those Indian split-ups, that Chinese family fighting at every generation, the English primogeniture system all ensure that individuals at each generation can have their own dreams. In modern multigenerational wealth management, that individualization usually occurs traumatically but need not. And it usually occurs through complete separation, but it need not.

In fact, every few years and certainly every generation, the fossil should be split open to see what is inside. The family wealth management structure should be reexamined. Discard the notion of family altogether in that reexamination and look instead at individuals and their needs. If that is done purposefully and well, the efficiencies of scale achieved by keeping the wealth bundled can exist together with the harmony.

Two very different situations can offer insight. An Asian family, in its fifth or sixth generation of wealth, had one branch, five siblings, in a family office. That branch had split from the rest of the family in a dispute over the family business and had ended up owning the family business after bitter court fights. The branch itself, the five siblings, had resolved its own subsequent disagreements over the family business through the purchase by one sibling of the business. The family office represented a complete bundling of services and ownership, even though only one of the siblings, with his son, had any interest in the family business.

The enlightened leadership of that Asian family office had handled what would have surely been a bitter dispute relating to the family business. By building and managing a conversation and process, the leadership guided the family through division of the assets so that the brother interested in the business owned the business and the others owned portfolios unrelated to the business. The family philanthropy remained centralized for them all, but the process and the conversation about "unbundling" also resulted in several independent foundations for some of the siblings. Investment management, accounting, legal services, cash management services, and "concierge" services all remained bundled. The family office continued to manage affairs for each sibling, but each had considerable independence.

A family of similar lineage but without a family business had had its affairs run by a senior member of the family, the family wealth steward. He was father and uncle to five children, with the able assistance of a senior family office executive and a staff of four or five. When the wealth steward died, the family office executive (then 90 years old) took control. He called regular "family office board meetings," where he sat at the head of the table and called the children "the boys and girls" even though they were in their midfifties at the time. If any wanted cash, he or she had to go to the 90-year-old with justification for the request. The 90-year-old asked all the children to sign blank tax returns before the returns were prepared— "confidentiality, you know." At these so-called family office board meetings the tension became palpable. Some of the adult children would be physically sick before or during the meetings, and relationships between them began to deteriorate. The family office executive exercised the authority of the deceased wealth steward and the level of respect required of the children forced them to fight with each other rather than with him.

That family office effectively collapsed. The children decided that notwithstanding taxes and costs, the wealth should be unbundled. A lengthy and costly process resulted in each family member going his or her own way. Within a year, their family relationship had improved and each felt independent. Efficiencies were clearly lost but freedom was found. The eldest joyfully described the experience: "I feel like a bird freed from a cage!" She had found freedom through recognition of her own individuality—truly freedom from wealth.

To respect the importance of the individual, every family wealth management program must begin with and regularly engage in a conversation with each adult member of the family ultimately to determine where he or she wants independence and where he or she does not care. It must be clear that neither the *legal* nor *equitable* ownership of wealth can be owned by a group other than through systems of control and sharing of benefits. Systems and sharing work best when everyone has what he or she needs.

Most people do not care who prepares financial statements and tax returns and other bookkeeping and accounting chores, so long as they are done competently and well supervised. Most do not care what lawyer is taking care of structuring and other legal issues. Most do not care who is managing their assets, but most do care whether the portfolio is aggressive or conservative. Many care what gifts are made and to whom. Many care what charities are to receive grants. Most care where they take vacations and how they relate to siblings.

If the family bundles against the wishes of one or two members, they come to resent the bundling even of what they would not otherwise mind. So if asset allocation is bundled within the family, members may resent the managers actually selected, whereas if goals and objectives are individualized, which managers implement those goals may be irrelevant. And if gifts, philanthropy, and vacations are bundled, the family members will fight the bundling of those and everything else.

The exercise necessary to avoid the conflict is meeting with individual family members as if they were not family members and had nothing in common. That is a fiction, of course, as they may share trusts and genetics and background. What are they willing to combine to create "business efficiency"? Let us emphasize the "business" part of that since sentimental family harmony may be one member's meat and another member's poison. The family can often achieve business efficiencies through strategic bundling without sacrificing independence if, but only if, they bundle only those services and products where members do not care about independence. A family can achieve harmony much more effectively through this kind of analytic approach. And, if some members of the family want to focus attention on family matters to create harmony they should consider voluntary family reunions, histories, and social gatherings, albeit possibly managed by the family office.

Individualization is not easy. There are business considerations and economic efficiencies to bundling for financial services providers and family offices. The financial services industry builds efficiencies of scale into bundling and, possibly more importantly, through bundling makes changing a financial services provider much more difficult because change appears to require some kind of functional process of selection effectively to include all members of the family. Keeping everyone together keeps assets under management and ultimately reduces the number of services that a family requires, but most of the family members are captives to the bundle.

For a family office, bundling can be crucial since, with the costs of the family office fixed, a reduction of assets under management increases the percentage cost of those remaining. So long as primogeniture is not the norm, usually each generation increases the number of family members and reduces the assets held by each. This is sometimes called the "per stirpes" disbursement of wealth. If a member is "freed from a cage," his or her assets are no longer part of the pool and the costs of the others are increased.

Yet, there can be no functional management of family wealth so long as the wealth holders—or any of them—feel imprisoned. Without a sense of independence and freedom, family members will treat the most insignificant issue as a battleground in the ultimate war for freedom. I have seen a family disintegrate over the selection of the interior decorator for the family office. I have seen anger and fury over whether the family meeting will be held in the morning or the evening. I have seen a family in protracted battles ending in court over the disposition of Aunt Lizzie's teapot, when hundreds of millions of dollars get divided by the family without conversation. The issues are not the decorator or the time of the meeting or the teapot. The issues are described as issues of "principle"; they are really issues of independence and self-actualization.

The executive director of a large family office in England was explaining that the policy of the office was to run all portfolios identically. In fact, all were pooled together and family members simply had interests. Family members (of which there were hundreds) were not welcome in the office and were not expected to talk to family office employees. Any interaction was required to be through the chairman, a senior family member, and office hours were limited. A family member's only options were to stay in the pool or to pull out entirely. I asked the executive director why this arrangement was better for a family member than an interest in a generally available partnership or mutual fund run by Goldman Sachs, where one could redeem part if not all, investment was professionalized, and the pool to work with might be larger and facilitate better due diligence. "Our fund reflects the culture of the family" was his reply. Not sure what he meant, I asked him whether there was belief that the family members all shared an identical culture. "That is what family wealth is all about," he replied. Culture, dreams, and individuality all merged into a single investment pool in his mind.

I introduce myself as Charles Lowenhaupt when I meet a person. I do not introduce myself by saying, "I am a Lowenhaupt; incidentally my first name is Charles." I have found no culture where every family member has exactly the same name—that would be too confusing. And, in most cultures, a name or combination of names is distinctive, individual by individual. If I were a member of that British family where all assets are pooled ("take it or leave it"), I might resent my identity being marginalized. My resentment would color my view of performance, my relationship with the chairman and the executive director, and my perspective on family wealth.

From these examples we can see that building any family wealth management program must start with the understanding that each individual will have his or her own personality, culture, needs, aspirations, and understanding of what the wealth is for. Only by taking each individual into account can one serve a group. One must free each bird from the cage of family before the flock can travel together.

4

The Importance of Comfort

IF ONE'S DESTINATION IS FREEDOM FROM WEALTH, THE ROAD MUST be one of comfort. Without freedom, comfort is difficult to achieve, and without comfort, freedom is impossible. In building a sound wealth management program, every wealth holder must start by building a comfortable relationship with the wealth. Yet many wealth holders in the United States, Europe, and Asia are painfully uncomfortable with their wealth. The wealth becomes a source of anxiety, not comfort.

How does one build comfort in a relationship with wealth? The answer might start with an understanding of "biophilia." E. O. Wilson articulates that theory of biophilia, a manifestation of which is a "preference for certain natural environments as places for habitation." Modern people everywhere, writes Wilson, "wish their home to perch atop a prominence, placed close to a lake, ocean, or other body of water, and surrounded by a park-like terrain" (*The Naturalist*, page 360). We want to see trees with spreading crowns. In another publication he notes, "The location is today an aesthetic choice and, by the implied freedom to settle there, a symbol of status. In ancient, more practical times the topography provided a place to retreat and a sweeping prospect from which to spot the distant approach of storms and enemy forces" (*The Diversity of Life*, page 350).

Wilson goes on to offer the following example: "Consider a New York multimillionaire who, provided by wealth with a free choice of habitation, selects a penthouse overlooking Central Park, in sight of the lake if possible, and rims its terrace with potted shrubs. In a deeper sense than he perhaps understands, he is returning to his roots" (*The Naturalist*, page 361). For that New York multimillionaire, life with the kind of sweeping prospect that gave his ancestors comfort remains the lifestyle that gives him or her comfort.

The biophilia theory takes us back to our roots on the savannahs of Africa, where from a plateau our ancestors could see predators coming, could easily find a source of water and food, but could also be near the shelter of trees and caves. In this same vein, whether in Hong Kong, New York, or Sydney, an apartment with a large window and view out over the water is always most comfortable.

What does biophilia have to do with wealth management? Simply stated, wealth holders need a clear perch from which they can see and understand all threats and from which they can see where they may want to go. They want a familiar landscape with sustenance visible.

Quite often, wealth holders do not enjoy the comfort of a privileged perch on a high bluff because their financial and other service providers have made their lives unnecessarily difficult. Attend a family wealth program anywhere in the world, whether through the Institute for Private Investors, Family Office Exchange, Campden, or another, and you will find a nervous tension in the room. You will see many there jump from attention to the speaker to iPhone or BlackBerry. Some will bite their nails and otherwise exhibit signs of discomfort. They are feeling surrounded by those who know what they do not know or understand. They worry that stewardship or protection of their family wealth requires that they know what they do not know. And those who believe they have figured out what they need to know are eager to share successes with the others. So much to learn, so much to worry about, and so little capacity!

The novelist George Eliot has been attributed with the following passage about comfort:

> Oh, the comfort, the inexpressible comfort of feeling safe with a person, having neither to weigh thoughts nor measure words, but pouring them all out, just as they are, chaff and grain together,

certain that a faithful hand will take and sift them, keep what is worth keeping, and with a breath of kindness blow the rest away.

Comfort is not easy in the valley of the wealth management conference. Comfort begins with security, consistency, and minimized surprises. Absence of fear (whether of loss, bad news, or the unknown) will bring comfort. Harmony in family and business promotes comfort. Reliable relationships with family, business associates, and advisors are helpful in gaining comfort.

Distrust and fear are impediments to comfort. Lack of control or understanding can create anxiety and discomfort. What you do not know or understand makes you uncomfortable because it is hard to relax in the presence of uncertainty and threats unseen.

I have yet to attend a family wealth conference where I see a comfortable audience. Questions asked most frequently include those searching for the "ideal" model, asking whom to trust, and looking for tools to create functionality out of dysfunction. I am often asked "What is the best governance structure for a family?" as if there is a best remedy for family dysfunction just as there may be a best remedy for a fallen soufflé. The questioner assumes that there may be a secret model known to everyone but himself or herself. Of course, there is no secret remedy. Until the "ideal" family is created and produced consistently, there can be no "ideal" governance structure.

There is no secret model to gain comfort. How to become comfortable with wealth requires analysis of what is making you uncomfortable.

That analysis is made difficult by the financial services industry, which builds opaqueness and obfuscation into its operations. Unfortunately, complexity is a built-in part of the industry's "product mix"—investments, tax analysis, and fundamentals of custody, counterparty risk, and financial analytics. Correctly perceiving that the industry is putting on the hard sell, clients are inclined to distrust, and that causes discomfort. To resolve the distrust, clients try to understand details and pierce the opaqueness, but understanding details and piercing opaqueness is often nearly impossible. Individuals then feel they do not know what they do not know. Wealth holders have no clear view of where risks may be or how to analyze risk, and they feel threatened by the unknown.

Let's approach the issue of discomfort resulting from the financial services industry's practices from another perspective. A jet is just as complex and just as opaque as any hedge fund. The transportation regulatory framework is even more difficult to understand than the securities framework. A jet flight is just as subject to disasters as any wealth management program. One has no control whatsoever over the operation of an airplane. Yet, why can we board a flight in Los Angeles and get off in Sydney without feeling we must understand how to navigate the plane ourselves? In neither case can you know every detail and understand all systems and elements. However, when wealth holders meet a financial services provider, they often feel they must trust him or her before they can do business together. We rarely meet our jet pilots, and yet we put our lives in their hands.

What is the difference between that portfolio management and that transpacific flight? Simply stated, we know that there are proven, established processes providing objective protection of every passenger on that flight—from training of pilots to maintenance of mechanical systems to language to be used to emergency procedures. And we know those processes evolve from years of experience and wisdom.

It stands to reason then that comfort is necessarily derived from process and wisdom. We can get comfort from a commanding view showing us everything we may fear. The wisdom to know what we don't know, to seek help from those who do, and to create the proper process to ensure the smooth takeoff and delivery is the equivalent of commanding heights. This wisdom is the plateau from which we can overview and ensure that we are looking at a forest but can discern the threats to us. The wisdom creates the comfort that significant wealth owes to the wealth holder.

Blind trust alone should not provide comfort in wealth management any more than in air travel. But the industry of wealth management exalts trust; it does not demand process and discipline of its clients because discipline and process would remove the sense of complexity and powerlessness that requires customers to pay so much for so little. People trusted Madoff, Lehman, Weavering, AIG, and so on. Trustworthiness is the garb of the scoundrel who can sell his fraud, so long as he is clothed with trust.

While wisdom helps build the process and therefore the comfort, it's also important in grounding strategy to ensure that every action will lead to a goal. As the capacity to look out over the forest to the river gives us the view of what we need to see—our water supply—and as our jet ticket says clearly that we want to go to Sydney, so we must know where we want to be to help us build the wisdom to get there. We must know what the wealth is for to make sure we can decide how to make it do its job. We must have the perspective of the height to allow us to see over the trees and to the water beyond.

The wise counselor, the trusted advisor becomes key here by helping analyze decisions in terms of goals. His or her wisdom can help us see the places we should not be comfortable because they do not get us where we are going. What risks should we take to help us move along our path, and what risks should we not take as they do not relate to where we are headed? The wise counselor helps us with perspective, and this help is often merely a question of pointing out the obvious.

The following three examples illustrate how wisdom helped three wealth holders make better decisions for themselves and their families. In each case, the wealth holder was prepared to be comfortable without the aid of a commanding view derived from wisdom. You will see how, in each case, a touch of wisdom allowed a perspective akin to that on the heights of biophilia.

+ A 90-year-old American, predicting the demise of modern society and the Armageddon to follow, confided that he was stashing tens of millions of dollars of gold in more than 30 Swiss safe-deposit boxes. This plan allowed him to sleep well at night and gave him great comfort. "I am secure and my family is secure no matter what," he said. I asked him who knew of these boxes besides himself and whether he had told his son. "Oh no, I dare trust no one. The Communists might get my son and he might disclose the secrets." I then posed the simple question: What happens if you die (and he was an "if I die" type rather than a "when I die" type) or if you are incapacitated? He looked puzzled at first and then concerned. He suddenly realized that if he died, no one in the world would know he had the gold or where to find it. The next day he gave his son the inventory of boxes.

• A group of doctors came into our offices many years ago. They were going to invest in a tax shelter scheme in the business of hog farming. The tax deductions would be quite generous and projections were that the doctors would double their investments through losses and credits. The doctors carried two weighty prospectuses and set them at the middle of the table, asking my father for advice. My father, one of the nation's leading tax attorneys at the time, said he could read those prospectuses and charge thousands of dollars to do so. Before he did, he wanted to ask the doctors what they would think of a hog farmer investing in medicine as a tax shelter. The doctors retrieved the prospectuses and with thanks left the office.

• A client telephoned my father with what he considered a sound plan, one that made him very comfortable. That night he planned to pack a suitcase with cash in the millions and the next day he would meet a Swiss banker in Nassau. The bank had a plan that allowed the banker to take the cash, deposit it in the bank, and keep it so secret that the IRS would never find it. The client was planning to save millions of dollars in taxes. My father suggested the client come into the office immediately and meet with the two of us. He did and repeated that plan. My father said: "Sounds very clever. But if that Swiss bank is willing to cheat the IRS, might it be willing to cheat you?" The client abandoned the plan then and there.

Comfort cannot come from one plan or one scheme or one decision. Comfort comes with holistic vision, making sure that every element works with every other element, that the entire web of wealth management is integrated, strategic, and accomplishing its goals. Comfort comes when we know that every detail is designed to work in harmony with every other detail in carefully considered processes to take us from what the wealth is for to what we should be doing. Wisdom helps design the processes, wisdom helps us keep our eyes on the goal, and wisdom helps us understand when a specific plan should not give us comfort. Here then is the view we need from the bluffs overlooking the forest to the river beyond.

5

The Importance of Strategy: Overview

DELIBERATE STRATEGY IS CRUCIAL IN THE MANAGEMENT OF SIGNIFI-
cant wealth, yet strategy is often absent or only partially applied by
an individual or a family running its affairs. With no strategy, the
wealth holder is always chasing transactions, deals, or schemes and
often is hurt when the wrong one is caught. There may be strategies
for some elements and not for others, for estate planning but not
for investment management, for governance and not for education.
In fact, the best wealth management is the execution of strategies
all designed to complement each other and to accomplish overall
purposes.

In the chapters that follow, we look at various components of
wealth management in terms of strategy. We explore strategy for
each topic as well as the capacity to have strategies complementing
each other to accomplish purposes. We look at areas of philanthropy,
investment policies, capitalization, governance, family legacy and
values, and next generation education. In each, we uncover the components and discuss how careful design of strategy can help build a
cohesive program.

To understand why strategy is so critical in wealth management, this example may be instructive. One time, I was designing the ideal week in a northern Thailand spa. To begin, I started with some fundamental questions: why am I choosing that spa, what do I want out of it, and are there other sights I want to see in the area? Those are the questions I asked before I started planning the trip. Once I had answered them, I contacted the spa and designed the spa program that would meet my needs. Then I chose my flights and timing carefully to avoid snow in Chicago, to consider layovers and the likelihood of making connections (since if I missed one I may have lost my string of succeeding flights), and to find a place to rest for several days, possibly Bangkok or Singapore, to manage jet lag and exhaustion. I wanted those days of rest so that every day at the spa would be fully productive. I also had to plan my return flights to be as free of stress as possible with easy connections and airports not likely to be difficult to maneuver. I considered what I needed to pack, including what kinds of clothes, how many changes, what drugs for precaution, how many books, what the weather might be, and what would happen if I were delayed overnight in either direction. I confirmed that my health insurance was adequate to cover an emergency illness and that an illness before I traveled would not result in lost deposits. I looked at whether there were inoculations required or medications to take prophylactically. I considered how I could communicate with home—by computer, by phone, by mail— and what facilities would be available during my trip. I developed a cash supply, ensured my credit cards would be easy to use, investigated currencies and exchange rates, and ensured that any pressing bills could be paid from home while I was away. I considered what emergencies might occur in my absence requiring my involvement and left contact information with appropriate people so that I could be reached in an emergency. Finally, I arranged for transportation from my home to the airport.

I focused on all these details, each independent but all interrelated, to ensure that my week at the spa provided the rest and relaxation I was looking for. The goal—a good week at the spa—was clear; the strategic design and execution of each element required work. The result of the effort was that my week at the spa was all I had hoped for. "I had a wonderful week at the spa" was the full story on my return home.

Effective wealth management is no different from planning a successful trip to a spa in a far-off place. You need to start with a goal. The goal is the answer to the question, what is the wealth for? Whatever the answer to that question, the journey itself must be planned strategically individual by individual, not as part of some dynastic mandate or under predetermined family criteria. Once the goal is clearly understood, each element of the plan can be managed strategically and guided by wisdom and disciplined process. Every element of the plan of action must be designed, implemented, and monitored to accomplish the goal.

6

The Importance of
Strategy: Philanthropy

MAKING PHILANTHROPY A PART OF ANY WEALTH MANAGEMENT program is always—and I mean always—strategic. Indeed, I open this section on strategy with a discussion of philanthropy because I have never found a situation in which philanthropy should not be used to make the wealth do what it should do. If wealth's purpose has anything to do with living comfortably or recognition of family or building functionality in a community, strategically designed philanthropy can help achieve that objective. As it stands today, however, philanthropy has become a code word for building foundations and making charitable grants. In fact, it is actually a much broader concept and encompasses any engagement in community for the benefit of others. To understand the powerful effect philanthropy can have for a family, it is instructive to look at these examples.

A family, one apparently without great wealth, lost a child to illness in a children's hospital during the Christmas holidays. In every year since, family members, including mother, father, and remaining children, have spent the holidays at the hospital supporting other families suffering with ill children by bringing food, washing clothes, running errands, and providing emotional support. That family is using the family's experience and collective sensibility to help others in the community. In the process, that family is helping itself deal with grief and build meaning out of its loss. This philanthropic program is strategically furthering the family's functionality.

An Indian family business, very large and very successful, has a policy that any family member in the business must spend a certain amount of time each year as a volunteer providing social services to those in the small and impoverished village the family left to start its business more than 100 years ago. That is family philanthropy as well as corporate philanthropy. It strategically reinforces the family's identity and legacy.

Fifteen years ago, wealth holders in Hong Kong told me that philanthropy was not a part of their culture. Then I learned of many Hong Kong wealth creators who returned to their Chinese villages of origin to build schools, found hospitals, and provide other social services. Without foundations, tax benefits, and organizational infrastructures, these contributions to communities were not called philanthropy. But they fulfilled the strategic purposes of the family as effectively as some of the world's largest, best-oiled family foundations.

Philanthropy may be too technical a term for these purposes. That family working in the hospital would not have described its program as philanthropic. When I described the Indian family business policy of working in the village as philanthropic, the senior family member looked perplexed. "This is not philanthropy. We have a separate philanthropic foundation," he said. "This is simply a part of our business culture."

A Chinese advisor to several wealthy families in Beijing cautioned me never to use the term *philanthropy* with those families. "They resent the concept as too institutional and not entrepreneurial. They do not see it as comporting with Chinese culture." Instead he urged me to talk about how best to fulfill one's "duty." "That word brings understanding and an open heart to your conversation about community," he said.

For our purposes, *philanthropy* can be defined very broadly as engaging constructively in one's community, as a patron, as a donor, as a volunteer, or as one merely fulfilling duty.

When we talk about strategic philanthropy, we do not mean what the professional fund-raisers and the charities often mean, which is how to make your dollar raise more money for the charity or how to ensure that your dollar is best used by the charity. This often moves into social entrepreneurship. Those concepts and those perspectives have added great value to charitable programs and often allow the donor comfort as she or he makes gifts. But they are not what we mean now when we talk about strategic philanthropy.

Strategically, philanthropy should always be part of family wealth if the wealth's purposes include multiple generations or family legacy. If multigenerational wealth is for anything it seems that it should allow oneself, one's children, and one's grandchildren to live in a world that is at peace and where they need not fear for health and safety. No one wants to live in a world where people are dying in the streets from pneumonia. No one wants to live in a world where poverty is driving crime or ignorance leaves humanity without sensitivity. Everyone wants to live in a world with beauty, both natural and human created. Everyone wants to believe that diseases can be cured. All of these are reasons, strategic reasons, to use multigenerational wealth to support social services, education, public health, health research, the arts, environmental programs, and any number of other causes.

Further, philanthropy is by its very nature strategic in building family legacy and sense of family ties if you recognize that the line between community and family becomes thin as families become larger with each generation. Is there a fundamental difference between a sixth cousin and a neighbor not related by blood? At some point, does the family not transition into the larger community, and can one have commonality with another without responsibility for that person? On this basis, multigenerational wealth should have connection with community to be meaningful in terms of family.

Strategic philanthropy is how to make a philanthropic program help the wealth holder or the family accomplish its goals. There are numerous examples of this kind of strategic philanthropy.

Family Name

Perhaps the most visible use of strategic philanthropy is that by which the philanthropist effectively changes the public perception of the family name. As businesses became national in the mid-nineteenth century, robber barons with names like Rockefeller, Carnegie, and others developed a public respect for their names through charity, and today they are seen as community leaders and philanthropists. Consider Michael Milken, until recently one of the great rogues of Wall Street. He is now considered a solid citizen and the darling of Los Angeles by reason of his philanthropic and community engagement. In the mid-1990s, the name of Gates was globally synonymous with antitrust violations; today it is associated with bringing social and medical services to Africa. The Gates transformation was accomplished through a global philanthropic program and focused on the most distressed areas of the world.

Similar stories are unfolding worldwide. There is an Asian family where the patriarch built huge wealth and went to jail. His sons continue to run businesses, each firmly placed in a community and behaving with integrity and responsibility. But each member of the family shares a name with the patriarch; none wants that name associated with the crimes of the father. They will design a philanthropic program that touches each of their communities, that relates to the sins of the father, that ennobles the family name and allows each to live with pride in his community.

None of these legacy-altering uses of philanthropy develops casually. Each involves a careful and detailed design and implementation of a strategy to "rebrand" the name as it needs rebranding. It is no coincidence that the Gateses' effort was led by the father of Bill Gates, the Ford effort by the descendants of Henry Ford. Each has been highly successful.

In a world of global wealth the opportunities and benefits of strategic philanthropy are boundless. If as suggested by some there are 400 billionaires in China, imagine what names can be branded and what good can ensue. India cannot be far behind. Russian oligarchs are already starting to consider their images in early philanthropic efforts. The U.S. experience of frontier, ungoverned wealth creation of the nineteenth century led to America's becoming the unrivaled jurisdiction of philanthropy. Why should that not be the global experience in the twenty-first century, creating strategically branded names in country after country?

Functionality

Another effective use of strategic philanthropy can be building functionality within the family itself. Rebranding the family name alone will allow more functionality by each family member—"holding his head high in his community," as one wealth holder declared. But a family can also design a program strategically to build communication and strengthen relationships within the family itself.

Operation of a well-designed philanthropic program requires process and wisdom. Process is never intuitive in families since relationships started when the youngest member was an infant and the parent was the authority at mealtimes. To introduce process successfully, it helps to find a table around which the family can sit without the early emotional memories of the dinner table. Wise strategists frequently turn to philanthropy to encourage process in the family relationship without personal concerns about economics and with focus outside of the family itself. Philanthropy can work to encourage that functionality if the philanthropy is designed strategically.

A good example of that principle is a wise woman who was managing most of the investment processes of the wealth created by her deceased husband. She was working directly with the bank managers of the wealth as cotrustee even as her three children, all in their forties, were leading lives actively engaged in careers and interests unrelated to the wealth. How should she start to transition the wealth governance from herself to the three children? Their relationships with each other were not particularly functional, yet many of the trusts and partnerships were to be shared interests of all of them.

Her decision was to form a charitable foundation—a large one. She would divide it into three separate pools, and the governance of each of those pools would reside exclusively with one of the children. She herself would have no role and no child would be expected to collaborate with another. She gave no direction whatsoever and articulated no expectation other than that each child would be involved in giving to charity.

Within three years of creation of the foundation, the children concluded that they may as well build a common administration to manage paperwork, tax filings, and the like. They hired a very competent executive director who handled only "the paperwork." Recognizing the competence of the executive director, each child came to rely more and more on her to help with grant solicitation and evaluation, and within five years of creation, the three children came to realize that their gifts might be much more effective if they collaborated in considering and making grants. Under the guidance of the executive director, processes and communications were developed to allow the pooling of the philanthropic initiatives and the collaboration of the children. Within 10 years, all functions and decisions had become pooled and common. The last step taken in the foundation was the development of an investment process and policy that was collaborative and harmonized the foundation's history of interests with investment process.

Once the family members were working together with process and functionality in the foundation, they were indeed ready to move into full engagement together in the other investment portfolios and elements of the family wealth management program. Today, the matriarch's children are strategically designing programs in the foundation to engage their own children.

Why was that foundation so successful for that family? It was conceived and operated strategically. The matriarch deliberately removed any sense of control or forced bundling by playing no role herself in the foundation and by giving each of her children structural independence. The relative simplicity of making grants did not interfere with any child leading his or her life practically or emotionally. The foundation was ideal for this strategy because it took nothing away from a child, yet no child felt entitled to the assets in the foundation. No child felt he or she had to be a leader because none had to work with another. No child felt he or she had an economic stake in the foundation, and none felt that there was any evaluation of investment or philanthropic performance. Family dynamics were completely removed. They were removed strategically and the foundation served its purpose: bringing to the family relationships a functionality to be used on pooled assets held elsewhere in the family. The foundation further resulted in each child's deriving the satisfaction of engagement in community. Today the children and the foundation are functioning well, and together they are helping to build community.

$$\underline{\hspace{3cm}}\left(7\right)\underline{\hspace{5cm}}$$

The Importance of Strategy:
Investment Policies

A FAMILY SHOULD DESIGN ITS INVESTMENT POLICIES, PROCESSES, and disciplines strategically to meet the family's goals and objectives. The challenge again is achieving the perspective necessary to see the destination before selecting the route to get there. Every element of investment theory, policy, and analytics should work together to make the wealth do what it is intended to do by helping the wealth holder accomplish his or her purposes.

We could examine individually and separately each of the elements we review in this chapter—performance measurement, volatility, transparency, asset allocation, diversification, investment styles, due diligence, and investment education; however, ultimately they must all be harmonized if they are to promote the purposes together. A family might examine each alone in terms of wealth preservation or wealth creation, but wealth is never for preservation or creation. Wealth is created or preserved to accomplish a specific purpose.

The success of an investment program is measured by its *appropriateness* to accomplishing its purposes, and, from this perspective, private wealth investment programs must be quite different from institutional investment programs. Compared to private wealth goals, institutional purposes are more consistent, pension fund to

43

pension fund, endowment to endowment, or institution to institution, and measurement of the appropriateness of the investment program of an institution is much better suited to analytic tools. The vocabulary, the evaluation, and the implementation of private wealth management programs are strategically different from those of institutions. This is because whether the investment program is "appropriate to accomplishing purposes" is necessarily different when dealing with private wealth holders. Although many of the topics and tools in the investment manager portfolio are standard solutions that look identically applicable to all investors, whether institutions or private wealth holders, few really are.

Let us look at several common ways in which private wealth and institutional wealth require completely different investment considerations. A family may design some portfolios for purely education or training purposes. Frequently, a private wealth holder will say that he or she wants a fund for "fun," whether high-stake risk, consumption, or acquisition of artwork. Taxation may be different for a private wealth holder so that the return produced by an investment may be different from gross return after taxes are taken into account. Time horizons will affect performance analysis, and the time horizon for legacy wealth is likely to be much longer than for institutional wealth.

As much as what is appropriate for an institution is not necessarily appropriate for a private wealth holder, what is appropriate for one private wealth holder is not necessarily appropriate for another. What the wealth is to accomplish, its purposes, varies from individual to individual. From those variations in purpose must follow variations in investment programs.

Returning to the foundation described in Chapter 6—which was strategically designed to be unbundled and, which after a while, was voluntarily bundled by the children of the creator—we had reached the point where family members, having pooled their grant-making and related activities, wanted to start to understand the investment of the endowment. The endowment had been managed by a bank. The foundation called a meeting for an analysis of the investment portfolio. Rather than starting with analytics of asset allocation and performance, we started with a review of the grant-making history of the foundation; areas of concentration were women, immigrants, and Jewish projects. But what does that have to do with investment? The answer quickly came with the review of industry weighting—double weight in oil companies. The oil stocks had done well, but were they consistent with the purposes and culture of the foundation?

The family moved from this conversation into designing a process to find investment managers who shared vision and views with family members. The proposition was that harmony of investment and goals is as important as investment return and that the foundation should reflect the values of the family members. Over a year, the foundation hired six or seven managers of different styles, mandates, and expectations but all sharing life views and principles with the family members. In this way, the foundation developed a harmony between its purposes and the investments.

Performance Measurement

When we consider investment performance we often consider return, that is, what percentage increase or decrease has occurred over the relevant time frame. The higher the increase, the greater the return. That is easy to measure mathematically. But any performance to be considered is only partly return; it is also *appropriateness*. For the pension or annuity fund, for the endowment fund, appropriateness takes into account the elements of risk and the requirements of return. For the private wealth holder, appropriateness takes into account whether the investments are appropriate in terms of what the wealth is for.

Appropriateness and dollar return may be completely different. A client created a charitable lead trust for his grandchild and future generations while the grandchild was an infant. Ten years after the grandfather created the trust, he and his son, the father of the child, ended up with no relationship with the child. Tragically, the mother had taken the child out of the country and he was completely estranged from his father. With no connection to his grandchild, the trust creator wanted to terminate the trust, but that was impossible. He was a very smart investor and asked me how he could take away the value of the trust from his grandchild and his grandchild's descendants. I asked him to name the worst investment he could imagine and he said that would be bonds. Bonds were a perfectly legal investment for a trustee, so the trustee built a portfolio entirely of long-term bonds, which has lost relative value over the 25 years since. The investment return of that trust looks terrible; the investment performance is just right!

Measuring performance is not easy if performance is defined as encompassing appropriateness. Technology can easily measure return on a portfolio and may even measure risk in a meaningful way. For a private wealth holder, when risk is only a part of appropriateness, many subjective considerations that cannot easily be measured may be applied.

That point was illustrated by one Hong Kong family that decided its investments should reflect family culture and values. Each portfolio, the family decided, should be evaluated in terms of its effect on a community and its reflection of the family's view of its role in the world. That seems a laudable standard for performance and clearly reflects a shared vision of what the wealth is for. However, the family is facing a challenge it will have trouble meeting—developing metrics and evaluative tools to reflect the performance taking into account family values. The definition of performance for that family is sound and wise; the desire to develop objective tools to measure the subjective standards may in fact be too ambitious.

It is difficult to measure return unless there has been a strategic analysis of the purposes of the wealth. Shall return be measured in terms of U.S. dollars as if none of the uses for the wealth may be outside that currency? Should non-U.S. residency, travel, investment, and philanthropy be disregarded in measuring performance?

I was reminded about the strategic value of managing currency risk by an experience I had in the late 1970s. A U.S. resident, I decided to invest in some Japanese stocks, while at the same time a Japanese friend decided to invest in some U.S. stocks. Several years later, the S&P 500 Index was up dramatically, the Nikkei 225 had been stagnant, and the dollar had slumped considerably against the yen. My Japanese friend reported that his investments in the U.S. stocks had been lackluster; however, I found that my Japanese investments had soared. Measuring return in yen produced a quite different result from measuring return in dollars.

Volatility

Almost any wealth creator has faced substantial volatility during the creation of wealth. And long-term wealth preservation has encountered the vicissitudes of markets as they go through depression and recession. Mechanical tools for implementing and guiding standard models of strategy attempt to collar volatility but are not always perfect.

Technology and analytics have developed "Monte Carlo" programs to measure and test risk tolerance. They are relatively easy to use, and they create enough data that most users feel the comfort of process and technology, even if they do not quite understand what the data mean. The programs give the advisor a complete booklet and easy tools for communication. All in all, the computer gives a standard analysis that sets forth the "reasonable" terms of tolerance for volatility.

But consider some of the faulty assumptions and conclusions that can occur with these kinds of programs. Reducing volatility through utilization of derivative products and funds of funds may or may not work. The assumption that there can be fail-safe, absolute return strategies will continue to prove erroneous. And many would consider lack of transparency risky, but that risk is not measured.

Several individuals in a family of wealth created early in the past century and enhanced over 80 years of investing in common stocks had moved from a traditional large-cap growth manager to a more "modern" manager of managers and developer of funds of funds. Over two or three years, Monte Carlo exercises had moved them into funds of funds and lowered expected volatility. With the realization that tax reporting would be delayed because of the complexity of the funds of funds, the family members began to feel uncomfortable. In essence, the lack of transparency was bothersome. Analyzing their goals as long term and their objective as feeling comfortable with their wealth, they determined that they really did not mind volatility and made the strategic decision to move out of funds of funds and back into portfolios of common stocks, diversified as to style and manager. Shortly after moving out of the less volatile funds, the portfolios went through the downward plunges of 2008; their owners were not fazed or worried. They were comfortable with the decision they had made and the resulting portfolios.

Indeed these individuals concluded that volatility was not bad. Others cannot tolerate any volatility and should consider portfolios that are fixed somehow in value (not easy but clearly a sound objective to try to accomplish). The reasonable conclusion is that there can be no "standard" evaluation of appropriateness with respect to volatility. The technology available for these purposes is not complete since it cannot have the conversation to ascertain feelings about volatility.

Transparency

Like volatility, transparency requires individualized consideration. Opaqueness may be appropriate in some situations and not in others. Consideration must always begin with analysis of how transparency or opaqueness strategically furthers the purpose of the wealth.

Definitions of transparency are already somewhat confused, so before evaluating whether transparency is desired, it is useful to define it. A banker assured me that his bank's proprietary fund of funds was "fully transparent." Did that mean that as a trustee owning that fund of funds I could know what the various managers held? He explained that I could not know that, though I could know that his bank put the fund of funds together. Then perhaps the bank could tell me what the underlying managers owned; but no one at the bank knew the names of the various underlying funds. Each fund manager knew what he owned, I was told. Transparency? The banker replied: "It is derivative transparency."

Regardless of the definition, investment transparency has not been required through most of modern times. Most customers have been willing to live with opaqueness over the past decade—look at the chicanery nicely hidden in Lehman, AIG, Madoff, and others. The current insistence on transparency is partially a reaction to the widely publicized frauds of 2008 and 2009 but will take considerable effort to maintain in a world of derivatives, private equity, and alternative investments.

As a strategic matter, transparency should be viewed as inherently neither good nor bad. Instead it should be seen as an element of process. Can the process being developed so that wealth serves its purpose also be consistent with funds, strategies, and other investments that cannot be understood or independently evaluated because they are not transparent? Are hidden fees and charges acceptable in making the wealth accomplish its purpose?

If wealth is for comfort and helping future generations be functional and free from the burdens of wealth, there must be an underlying assumption that the wealth holder *can* understand what is happening and how profits are being made whether or not he or she decides to do so. It is human nature to want to feel that we can understand what others are doing for us, even if we do not want to do it for ourselves. We educate our children to know how to use a sophisticated calculator, even though we may not expect them in adulthood to be engineers. We know enough to understand the auto mechanic as he describes the repairs that must be made even if we cannot make the repairs ourselves.

So if wealth is multigenerational and about functionality, transparency becomes important. If it is instead about control or protection, transparency may not be so important if the trustees and other stewards can evaluate investments adequately without transparency.

Asset Allocation

A strategy governing asset allocation is particularly important because the primacy of the asset allocation is one of the fundamental tenets of the wealth management industry. A poorly managed asset allocation strategy can lead to disaster. Conventional investment wisdom is that asset allocation plays a substantial role in determining investment performance. If we measure performance by appropriateness as well as return, we must consider asset allocation strategically and as reflective of appropriateness for the wealth holder.

There is an assumption in the wealth management industry that there exists an ideal asset allocation that can then be tweaked through a Monte Carlo simulation. In other words, what makes sense for the large pension or superannuation fund will make sense for most private wealth holders.

That assumption is almost always wrong. Any well-run pension fund or institution starts by looking at obligations and reserves. Before there can be any consideration of asset allocation, individuals must analyze what they need where to make the wealth do for them what they want it to do. Careful plotting of cash needs should be built into a piece of the portfolio, and that piece should be seen as free of any consideration of asset allocation—that is, free of the constraints of percentages in cash and fixed income.

If community is part of the purpose of wealth, it would not be unreasonable for a wealth holder to set aside a portion of a portfolio in clear liquidity to be used for charitable or private gifts, private investments in socially worthwhile projects or a friend's venture, or merely as "play money." All of this must be removed from the pool subject to asset allocation before any discussion of allocation can take place.

Consider a charitable lead annuity trust, a trust that has a fixed obligation to pay a fixed dollar annuity to charity for 30 years. In its earliest years, before there has been appreciation adequate to assure the annuity can be paid, the reasonable trustee will build a laddered reserve of bonds designed to pay the annuity for some reasonable term. The balance of the portfolio can then be subject to an asset allocation exercise.

Strategic design of a portfolio thus starts long before asset allocation. And it starts with understanding goals.

It may also start with understanding where the wealth has come from. Wealth coming from 80 years of a common stock portfolio should not move too rapidly out of that portfolio if comfort and legacy are to be considered. And wealth coming from 80 years of real estate should not move too quickly into common stock. That means at a given time, a portfolio of 90 percent equities can make sense for one person while a portfolio of 10 percent equities can make sense for another. Neither percentage comes from a hard-and-fast rule that should apply to every investor. Each reflects a notion of appropriateness designed for the particular investor.

Diversification

The importance of diversification is seen as comparable to the importance of asset allocation in any traditional analysis of an investment portfolio. Most investment experts see diversification as sound investment strategy, protecting against risk in almost all circumstances. Indeed, diversification can protect against some risks in all circumstances if it is broadly defined to include not only diversification of asset class but also diversification of currency, custodians, jurisdictions, liquidity, managers, and lifestyle capacity, all as we discuss in the following pages.

Diversification is commonly defined as spreading investment portfolios over many asset classes and many styles. But broadening that definition may be desirable in any strategic analysis. If the goal of diversification is protection against external risks, market risk is only one of those. A simple definition that includes only asset classes and styles limits the protective capacity of true diversification. Diversifying asset classes even among stocks and bonds is, of course, protective. But protection is enhanced when diversification is broadened to include different types of stocks and different kinds of bonds. Further protection can come with developing strategies to own assets other than stocks and bonds. Risks of custody, geopolitical developments, swindlers, and other factors can also be minimized through different forms of diversification.

Generally, wealth creators are not diversified during their creative period. As a general proposition, a great fortune is built on a great company. There are exceptions in conglomerates, such as Berkshire Hathaway and in the financial services business, but the world is filled with very wealthy individuals and families who built their wealth as did the Gates family, on one company in one jurisdiction. It is no surprise that diversification frequently begins when another generation comes on and decides to *protect* the wealth. Wealth creation is never a purpose for wealth, but until the wealth is there, its creation is the natural inclination. Once the wealth exists, its purpose is more likely to be accomplished through *preservation*. Diversification is the hallmark of preservation.

A wealth holder may have a "core holding," a particular stock or other asset that represents a substantial part of the portfolio and may have been the source of the wealth. The starting question is whether diversification out of a core holding is strategic. In some cases, there can be more financial success without diversification. There are those of great wealth who do not diversify. There are businesses that stay in families for generations and provide wealth to family members for even longer.

A patriarch sold his gas stations to Standard Oil, and 60 years later his heirs continue to hold Standard Oil (now BP) as a substantial part of their portfolio (until recently almost 80 percent) notwithstanding advisors urging them to diversify. Ask why they have held on so long and the answer is a kind of guilty, "We just don't want to sell. We know it is not smart, but that is what we want." Keeping the stock gave the family comfort even many years after the patriarch's death. In fact, the family believed that with hundreds of millions of dollars in the company, the stock price could fall by half and the family would still have plenty. They felt they would never be uncomfortable holding the shares they had inherited.

Then came the Gulf of Mexico oil spill in the spring of 2010, and the BP shares started to plummet. With anxiety and great distress making the decision, the family sold the entire position. There followed a kind of quiet peace. The family had indeed lost something like half the wealth, but what was left was adequate for all the family's purposes and was worth exponentially more than the Standard Oil stock the patriarch received when he sold his gas stations. Importantly, unlike many families holding failing businesses, the family realized the importance of selling the BP stock before the loss might be complete.

The world is full of stories where the families are not quite as fortunate. Look at any failed company and you are sure to find shareholders who lost their wealth. Many family members are sunk in the process of holding a family business. I watched two trusts established at the same time, each directing that the trust estate hold the shares of the company given to the trust and not diversify. At creation, each trust was worth $2 million. Holding publicly traded shares of a family company, one was worth nothing 20 years later—the company had gone bankrupt. Holding publicly traded shares of a widely held company, the other was worth $60 million 20 years later. In either case, with complete diversification the trust would have been worth somewhat less than $60 million and somewhat more than zero.

There may be other reasons not to diversify out of the core holding. A reasonable analysis of what the wealth is for may include an interrelationship of family, business, and community. If that is what the wealth is for, diversification may be protective but may not be strategic. Consider the handful of family businesses worldwide that are in the fourth, fifth, or sixth generation and how strategy would have been foiled if the business had been sold in its first generation. Those family businesses, whether Ford, Cargill, Johnson Wax, or Rothschild, define the family and their communities. Retention of the business without diversification is strategically central to that definition.

Where the decision has been made that diversification will help the wealth do what it is for, the next strategic consideration will be in what ways to diversify. Each case will require its own definition of diversification.

There was a time when nearly every U.S. investor said that diversification meant a portfolio of U.S. large-capitalization stocks and bonds, possibly with a little real estate thrown in. Today, that view would be seen as old-fashioned. Indeed at last count, experts were bandying 30 or more asset classes required for diversification.

There used to be an interesting difference between the way the Fung family and the Fisher family invested, according to public accounts. The Fung family, based in Hong Kong, built its wealth sourcing plants in China for retailers and others looking to China for manufacture. The Gap, owned by the Fisher family, was one of those retailers utilizing the Fung operation. The Fungs wanted to invest in the United States. The Fishers wanted to invest in China. The Fishers built a portfolio of publicly traded companies, none of which were in the manufacturing business, to diversify their base. The Fungs built a U.S. investment banking operation looking for investments to be made in U.S. retailers in which the Fungs could help build value by using their understanding of manufacturing. Either approach is a kind of diversification. Neither is clearly correct and neither is clearly wrong. Both are clearly strategic, and both are efforts to diversify with respect to a core holding.

Defining diversification requires careful consideration of the wealth holder, his or her goals, and his or her situation. Stocks and bonds are adequate for many people. However, let's look at a number of areas where the sophisticated investor, particularly one attuned to globalism, might demand diversification beyond even asset classes.

Asset Class

We have touched on diversification of asset class—stocks, bonds, and cash equivalents—and will touch on it again when we discuss investment styles later in the chapter. This type of diversification is well accepted in investment theory, and volumes have been written on the subject. Selection of asset classes and allocation to those classes must be strategic in all respects to accomplish the wealth holder's purposes.

Cash

Most asset allocation models have a category of "cash" and most statements categorize short-term obligations and money market funds as "cash." Indeed, when an individual is designing a portfolio, he or she must start by building into it his or her cash needs.

But in today's world, we must start by asking, what is cash? Cash is fundamentally currency, and deciding what currency or currencies should be seen as "cash" requires strategic analysis of needs and purposes. An individual based in the United States would likely consider the U.S. dollar cash and the Thai baht a speculative investment. Would the Thai resident apply the same analysis? And what should a family with residents in both the United States and Thailand treat as cash?

For a family living in different jurisdictions around the world, cash is something different for each jurisdiction. It can be U.S. dollars for the U.S. person, sterling for the British resident, euros for the French resident, yen for the Japanese, and so on. In a world of wildly fluctuating exchange rates, there can be no "standard" currency for such a family. For those families with members residing around the world, a cash portfolio must be designed around the members in the various "currency jurisdictions."

Similar considerations of strategy should be applied to the family that resides in only one jurisdiction. Suppose we have a fully U.S.-based individual. That individual may travel overseas or may have assets and investments outside the United States, possibly mortgaged by debts in non-U.S. currency. The individual may have private equity commitments in currencies other than the dollar; and he or she may have philanthropic initiatives outside the United States that must be funded in currencies other than the dollar. The individual (or the individual's family) is no less likely to suffer loss in fluctuating currencies than the family with globally diverse residencies.

Once the currency is set, how to hold it may remain a problem. We have seen money markets "break the buck" as they become worth less than they are stated. We have seen "almost cash" auction rate securities locked away and not accessible. In some currencies, such as the U.S. dollar, bonds (such as treasury obligations) are in fact cash; in others, such as the euro, the money printers do not offer debt.

So even after the wealth holder determines what he or she needs in cash, defining it and figuring out how to have it are both difficult.

Custodian

The banking crisis of 2008 left many wealth holders asking whether reliance on one custodian was in fact wise. If cash must be diversified, logistically the securing and placement of it must be diversified. If Lehman and AIG, and other giants "too big to fail," could approach or enter bankruptcy, was it truly wise to have all eggs in one bank?

Some wise businesspeople may say their lending bank wants more business, so they will send it some custodial work. That is an appropriate business decision—strategic from a business standpoint. It may also be a wise investment decision to use several other custodians as well, particularly if the lending bank is small and not likely to be "too big to fail."

In considering custodians, a wealth holder must apply due diligence to determine the distinctions among custodians based on business organization, business model, and jurisdiction of incorporation. The old belief that banks are safer than brokers may be misplaced in a world where banks are brokers and brokers are banks; structural and auditing differences can exist between two companies in the same business so that in fact Schwab may be quite different from Fidelity with respect to security of assets held. Even after the due diligence is finished, the conclusions will not be clear. Then it becomes reasonable to have several custodians to protect against failure of one.

Jurisdiction

In diversifying custodians, it may seem logical to limit oneself to custodians in one's own jurisdiction, particularly if that jurisdiction is the United States. If that jurisdiction is South Africa, or India, or Indonesia, or many other countries, the limitation would seem unreasonable if you can foresee political instability or feel uncertain that you can locate several responsible banks in the country. In light of the developments of the past years, some wealth holders are saying it is unreasonable to use Switzerland as one's only jurisdiction. And if it is reasonable to diversify beyond Switzerland, is it not also reasonable to diversify beyond the United States?

The point is that real diversification may also require diversification of jurisdictions. If cash is to have diverse jurisdictions, custody must follow the cash. If a family holds real estate outside its home jurisdiction—for example, the French in South America—should they not diversify jurisdiction with respect to all elements of their wealth? If currency controls reenter the world's economic policies, should one place all of one's affairs in just one country? The answer most likely is no.

Are equities truly diversified if they are all traded on the exchanges of only one jurisdiction? If oil is to be part of a portfolio, is it reasonable to hold interests only in the United States, or might one look at Eastern Europe and the Middle East and ownership in more than one? Should gold be held in several jurisdictions?

The world's refugees, whether from the Holocaust countries, South Africa, China, or elsewhere, know how important it is to find a secure jurisdiction. Any Indian who lived through the years of India's tightly controlled economy knows the rewards of having business outside India. Those who left China in the 1940s know that ownership of real estate in Hong Kong provided economic freedom. Today, refugees or individuals who believe they may be refugees in coming years are concluding that one jurisdiction is not enough. Many wise investors are using custodians in different jurisdictions, looking at market exchanges in different jurisdictions, and considering asset location in different jurisdictions. If Iceland and Ireland and Greece can stumble, might not other countries disappoint?

Liquidity

To have truly diversified liquidity requires a diversified perspective on currency and a diversified perspective on custody. But defining diversification of liquidity will also require strategic analysis in other areas as well. Those who relied on auction rate securities as their portfolio of liquidity were disappointed. Those who relied on Lehman custody for liquidity outside the United States were also disappointed. Greek bonds have proven not as liquid in euro terms as the bonds of a country actually printing the currency will appear in terms of that currency. Gold is liquid only as long as it is held in an accessible place, only as long as you can withdraw and use it.

There are two gold stories that illustrate this point. One investor placed his gold in safe-deposit boxes around the world. His theory was that wherever he happened to be, he could access some of his gold. That will prove sound so long as the safe-deposit boxes remain open.

Another investor designed a "gold fund" with certificates that could be redeemed for gold in banks around the world. The fund looked solid until Lehman entered bankruptcy—Lehman was a counterparty central to the entire arrangement. "Who would have guessed that Lehman would go bankrupt?" lamented the investor.

Managers

Theoretically, diversification of asset class, jurisdiction, and liquidity is most effectively accomplished by diversifying investment managers. Let each manager have its own investment mandate based on asset type, style, and jurisdiction. Diversification of managers now seems well-accepted policy. Indeed any consideration of the history of investment management companies must recognize that there has always been a sense of specialization of analysts within each.

Whether and how a private wealth holder diversifies managers must be considered strategically. It is not easy to diversify managers without a sound due diligence process to analyze the managers individually and in relationship to each other. One must consider the following questions:

♦ Does the manager's philosophy seem sound and do you understand it?

* Is the manager's operation and history consistent with that philosophy or style?
* Does the manager do what it says it does?
* Are the manager's benchmarks reasonable?
* Will the manager understand the wealth holder well enough to customize his or her portfolio to meet that individual's needs?
* How do the manager's portfolios relate to one another?

This last point is particularly complex. It is easy to have one manager buying while another is selling or one manager hedging while another is buying. Many investors found that a number of their managers, even those of different styles, were holding the same securities, such as AIG or Enron, or utilizing the same counterparty, such as Lehman. Indeed, it may be that one investment manager can provide more diversification and less concentration than multiple managers if that manager is attentive to the needs for diversification and has sound internal due diligence process.

Effective diversification of managers requires hard work, transparency, and complete understanding of manager after manager. Substantial due diligence infrastructure must be in place if one is to gain strategic benefit from diversifying managers. Is the wealth holder willing to invest the time and effort to build or secure that infrastructure? Does the wealth holder have the capacity to insist on full transparency? If the infrastructure is to be outsourced, is the wealth holder willing to invest the time and effort in evaluating managers of managers or consultants, and are the "industrial-strength" consultants actually available?

These questions cannot be answered abstractly. Strategic considerations are central to determining the responses appropriate for each individual. Is the wealth really "for" the kind of hard busywork necessary to answer those questions? There are no shortcuts. Family after family has had to ask one of its members to devote years of his or her life to building or securing the infrastructure necessary for due diligence. Is diversification of managers worth the loss of time and the impediments to self-actualization?

For most wealth holders the sacrifices necessary to build due diligence are not worth the loss of time. A well-designed family office may be a solution. "Outsourcing" to consultants may be a solution.

Many have solved the challenge of diversifying among several managers by hiring one manager who is good and has a diversified approach to investing.

Lifestyle

Some of the wisest wealth holders have what may be termed a refugee mentality. Most are refugees who have escaped Hitler's Germany, Mao's China, South Africa, Rhodesia, Iraq, and elsewhere. Ask these wealth holders what wealth is for and most will answer clearly: Wealth is for protection and freedom to move wherever and whenever the need arises. If that is what the wealth is for, strategic thinking leads to diversification relating to where to root one's life: passports, homes, languages, and associations.

A refugee whose family escaped Hitler and who now lives in Switzerland has great wisdom. He is diversified in the most complete and traditional ways with respect to asset classes, jurisdiction, cash, liquidity, and managers. His children have been educated so they have associations and friends throughout the world—contacts to connect with regardless of what is happening in one part of the world or another. He owns seven or eight hotels around the world, each with an apartment that is his own, so that he can live anyplace in the world. Ask him whether these hotels are good investments and he will answer that they are "the best" because they guarantee him the freedom to move easily and at any time. In effect, he has strategically diversified those places he can live comfortably. He has a diversification of residences.

Investment Styles

Different investors have different investment styles. Here we are not talking about diversification of those styles (which often makes sense) but rather selection of a style that makes sense for you. Fundamentally, investments must make sense to the investor not in every detail but in assumptions about the world. Consideration of investment style requires a worldview.

This goes well beyond the analytic strategy necessary to find the "optimal" mix of styles for greatest returns or matching of risk tolerance accomplished through so-called Monte Carlo exercises.

Individuals' understanding of the world around them and how they relate to it becomes a key ingredient in any strategic consideration of investment style.

The fact that even a wealth holder without expertise in investment theory can make observations that help guide investment portfolio and styles can be illustrated with many examples of successful stock picking. For instance, a friend of mine was an early investor in Minnesota Mining because his wife liked Scotch tape. Another friend had a background in retailing and sourcing hardware and invested early in Home Depot. Doctors were some of the early investors in Amgen. In each case, everyday or professional experiences informed a view on which companies had good prospects.

Broader investment issues can be answered by the nonprofessional based on personal perspective. Questions like this are asked by clients and answered by professionals in many investment reviews: "Will health-care control affect drug stocks?" "Is the United States going to continue to be a world leader?" "Are United States auto companies as good as Japanese auto companies?" In fact, anybody reading a newspaper can answer those questions with as much expertise as a Ph.D. in economics. In that way, an investor can help shape his or her own portfolio of stocks.

Should an investor be a "value" or "growth" investor? A value investor looks for companies or opportunities he or she believes are undervalued in the market. A growth investor looks for companies or opportunities that have performed well in the past and that the investor believes will continue to do well in the future. If well articulated, the distinctions between value investing and growth investing aren't so hard to understand. "Do we look for the dark horse or do we find a horse riding well and jump on?" That is the way one investment professional told it to me some 30 years ago. And as inexpert as I was, I could express an opinion.

Other investment questions can similarly be addressed based on logic and experience. "Will the world continue to develop with fewer and fewer boundaries and with more and more transportation; and will the United States always remain on top?" If the answer is yes to the first and no to the second, a global portfolio is appropriate. "Are there indices that will measure what I need to make my wealth do what it is for?" If so, passive investments may be appropriate. "Am I looking for good stories to make investment performance comprehensible?" If so, passive investments are not appropriate.

Investment styles must also be reflections of a wealth holder's purposes. I recently heard of an arms dealer who collects and invests in textiles. Although I have not met the gentleman, I am willing to wager that his alter ego needs the investment in soft goods of beauty.

The Chinese family that wants to measure performance by impact on the community and by more than return probably should be looking at investment styles different from those of the Texas family whose wealth has been built in the oil industry. The family whose wealth comes from banking or investment services is likely to look at investment styles different from those whose wealth was built on real estate. A good bond manager is probably crucial for the family that is most comfortable in fixed income and not even worth considering by the family that is most comfortable with volatility. Consider again the different investment styles and strategies employed by the Fung and Fisher families mentioned earlier in the chapter.

Alternatives, Derivatives, and "Cutting-Edge" Investment Styles

A wealth inheritor "of the old school" sent his sons to the boarding school he had attended in Massachusetts. He got his sons into his alma mater college and pounded "old-fashioned" values into them. They were to be in his mold and in his image, one that went back three generations to his great-grandfather, who built the wealth and invested in stocks and bonds through most of the twentieth century. Yet, at the first trust meeting his sons attended, the father introduced young Wall Street men who were talking alternatives, derivatives, and other "cutting-edge" investments. Strategies were hedged, derivatives related to mortgages on stretched consumers, and one fund was invested with Madoff. Was this a strategic investment program? Did it forward the purposes and values the father was trying to instill? Probably not. If the father had been one of the pioneers of the computer industry, if his culture was new ideas and he was trying to instill creativity, the session may have been appropriate. Transparency, liquidity, and complexity should not have been the standards in this investment design; values, tried and true, patience, and perseverance were the values to be encouraged. They were not.

If wealth is about freedom, convoluted investment strategies are rarely strategic. There can be no process, little delegatable, and no likelihood that the wealth holder will fully understand what he or she is investing in. The complexity alone can deprive family members of feelings of freedom. Instead they spend time trying to understand what they cannot and feeling unsure whether they should trust those running the investments. How can a person pursue passions to self-actualization if he or she is busy in a maze of derivatives and jargon?

Socially Responsible Investments

Many investors now look to an investment approach sometimes called socially responsible (or responsive) investment (SRI). Closely related to this are the concepts of mission-based investing, ESG (environmental, social, and corporate governance), sustainable investing, and ETI (economically targeted investing). These concepts developed over the years in endowments and institutional portfolios as a way to align the wealth holder's values and worldview with investment strategy.

The concept is that investments can be made in companies that meet certain criteria for improving the world; there are indices, managers, and funds based on that concept. And there are investors, institutional and private, demanding that all of their investments be "socially responsible."

The challenges for the wealth holder are twofold: getting agreement with other family members on what constitutes SRI, and finding managers who are willing and capable of designing a custom portfolio that reflects the values and cultures of the wealth holder.

A family seeking socially responsible investing for its foundation was given a questionnaire to complete regarding what they considered socially responsible. Some felt nuclear energy was a "good" investment to relieve pressure on oil; others felt it was environmentally irresponsible. Some felt that investments in farming operations were constructive to provide food for the world; others saw those as harmful because they destroyed native habitats. And so the arguments went, and the family conversation finally collapsed in disagreement. The mere selection abstractly of the theme of the investments became a platform for political disagreements and a battleground for the family's dysfunction.

The family harmony was restored with the presentation of a different process, designed to reflect that each family member had individual needs and values. An investment manager review process was designed in which each family member was separately introduced to three or four investment managers. Each of those managers was an individual investing in his or her own portfolio and owning his or her own company. Each was selected based on some sharing of interests with the family member. For example, one family member was involved philanthropically with programs for disabled children, and she was introduced to a manager with his own disabled child and active community commitment to the cause of disabled children. Each family member selected several managers for family consideration, and then the family interviewed those selected. On the basis of objective criteria and process established prior to those interviews, five or six investment managers were selected. Each of those managers was seen as a friend of one or more members of the family, and all were sensitive to the feelings of the family members.

The value of the foregoing approach to "cultural fit" is that it becomes personalized to leave each family member feeling comfortable with the investments. The approach allows objective evaluation based on subjective input. Incidentally, it teaches the family members that investment professionals are real people, leading real lives, with real loyalties and substantial dedication.

Investment style needs to be looked at strategically first. Who are the wealth holders, what are their comfort levels, what are their values, and what do they want to accomplish with the wealth? These questions must be answered before one even starts to explore how to diversify investment styles.

Due Diligence

Any investment program requires due diligence to ensure that policies can be implemented with discipline. Performing due diligence is always daunting. The volatility, chicanery, and uncertainty of 2008 and 2009 have made that task seem almost impossible. Indeed, one might say that today due diligence is the gold standard of investment management. It has become the most important function to execute well to ensure the proper management of significant wealth. Due diligence is broader than simply investigating and monitoring investment managers. Due diligence in its broadest terms is ensuring that all assumptions are correct, that all assets believed to be owned are owned, that all risks are considered, and that all facts are as they are represented. The question to ask yourself is, "Have I considered every risk and do I have the information I need to evaluate every risk?"

The best performance in the world is worthless if you do not own the assets performing; Bernie Madoff's investment results could not have looked better. Unfortunately, the assets did not exist. The wealth holder must try to understand counterparty risk, that is, whether another party to the agreement (such as a bank) will not live up to its obligations. An investor built a brilliant gold fund in 2007 secure in every respect except that it relied on the solvency of Lehman.

The investor needs to be confident that reporting is accurate as the investor analyzes an investment. Without adequate due diligence, investment decisions are built on sands of information and assumptions that may not be solid. Currencies and reporting of values can be particularly treacherous. Whether tax and other reporting is accurate and verified is central to any compliance program.

The strategic question is how to build a system of due diligence that allows continuing and complete monitoring of all the elements of an investment program. To answer that question of how to structure due diligence, start with the timeless and central question, what is the wealth for? Few wealth holders can say that what their wealth is for is "to allow me to perform the hard work of due diligence." Even those who enjoy the chase of a good investment, the challenge of building a successful investment strategy, will consider the due diligence process lackluster and uninteresting.

If a wealth holder is willing to rely on one manager and one custodian, due diligence can be fairly simple by examining the security of the custodian and relying on insights of the manager to understand and follow the goals of the client. But if a wealth holder wants to build a more complex investment program, how should that person provide for due diligence? One option is to build a complex, expensive, and less-than-adequate due diligence process by hiring staff to perform the due diligence. There are some huge single-family offices that have many employees performing various elements of due diligence.

Alternatively, the wealth holder can outsource due diligence. Just as many of the world's largest institutions hire consultants to perform investment due diligence, a wise wealth holder might outsource that role in some way. Any outsourcing should be to companies that are completely unconflicted and who have the bulk of asset base to build the infrastructure necessary. In other words, outsourcing of due diligence should be to an independent and large consultant. Once standards for selection are in place—such as independence, depth of capability, and investment perspective—the provider may itself be the subject of due diligence. However, that due diligence will be primarily to confirm that the clear standards are met and maintained.

Strategic analysis leads to the following conclusion: There are really two elements to investment advisory work, understanding the investment and understanding the investor. Family offices, whether single or multifamily, are ideally suited to understanding the investor. The size of the family office and its relationship with the client allow an intimacy that is conducive to understanding goals and monitoring them. But although a family office may be equipped to consider the investor, it may be less equipped to consider the investment or to perform the heavy-duty due diligence required. For that fundamental due diligence, a company with hundreds of billions of dollars under management can afford to build due diligence infrastructure much more completely than any to be built by even the largest family office. If freedom from wealth and comfort are considered central, for a complex portfolio is it not more strategic to avail oneself of the highest standard of due diligence in investing rather than to look for shrewd, agile, and small investment advisory services? And is it not wise to combine that industrial-strength investment capability with the smaller, more capable family office to understand the investor? Is relying on industrial-strength wisdom to perform investment due diligence not the way to create the comfort needed?

Finding the expert in investment—due diligence—is not easy for the private wealth holder. Unconflicted consultants with the infrastructure large enough to build a complex process of due diligence are difficult to locate. In fact, there are probably no more than five or six in the United States and far fewer elsewhere. If investment policy demands opaque and complex programs, due diligence requires the ideal investment consultant. When that ideal consultant cannot be accessed, then pragmatic considerations become the strategic reason to simplify the investment program. Selecting the right investment program starts with consideration of what level of due diligence can be found. If there is an "industrial-strength" consultant available, the program can be intricate and complex if that is desired. If a consultant is not available, simplicity, even mutual funds or long stocks and bonds, may be ideal. That's not because those "vanilla investments" will provide the best abstract performance but rather because they do not require an unattainable understanding of complex diligence issues.

One family office I was acquainted with designed the ideal investment program for the family. It was to be built around alternatives and derivatives, but with a portfolio much smaller than would be of interest to an institutional, independent consultant. The family found that it could hire consultants who built funds of funds, others who were owned by manufacturing companies, and others who had ties to specific products. That family decided, quite reasonably, to modify its investment program by hiring four or five managers who bought only stocks and bonds; and they found a fine, small, independent consultant willing to work for them to find and monitor those managers and confirm that custody. They designed their portfolio around what was possible rather than around what was ideal. That was strategic to help them achieve their purposes.

Investments as Education

A father recently decided to search for new investment managers for the family portfolios after many years of reliance on a large bank. He concluded that as his 21-year-old son became interested in investing, he could engage his managers to help develop his son's understanding. He set out certain requirements strategically designed to accomplish his purposes of educating his son. He wanted each manager to be a small company, an individual or individuals governing their own fates, building their own businesses, and fully invested in their businesses. He wanted each to be a "full" person with passions and interests beyond the investment business. He wanted each manager to be willing to talk about himself or herself, the process used in selecting investments, and the hard work of being in the investment business. Managers were selected and interviewed. In each, the son saw hardworking, disciplined, and process-oriented real people who rose and fell with their own investment decisions. Each was his or her own master and each lived the consequences of his or her decisions.

The selection process itself taught valuable lessons to the son. First and foremost, the son learned that investment management is a profession. Picking stocks and managing a portfolio was not an avocation that a person could dabble in. Managing money is a difficult and time-consuming business, and that is an important lesson. Next, the son saw that entrepreneurship is hard work with its ups and downs. Real people have real lives, and business and life take place together. Sometimes, coordinating life and complex work can be difficult. Finally, the son learned a bit about investment theory from people who were passionate, principled, and wise.

Another story also helps illustrate this point. A family whose wealth came from entrepreneurialism and continues to be built on entrepreneurialism is considering a private equity fund to be run by members in their 20s and 30s. The family will place a substantial amount of money in the fund, will hire a professional private equity expert, and will allow the younger family members to guide the fund as directors. The primary strategic purpose of the fund is not to produce investment return; it is instead to teach the younger members of the family about business. The first lesson to be learned is that starting a business and running it requires discipline and very hard work; the second lesson is that nine out of ten businesses will fail; the third and overarching lesson is that one does not "dabble" in investing, in entrepreneurship, or in business.

Are the foregoing strategies *investment* strategies or *next generation education* strategies? The answer is that they are both. A good strategy helps accomplish all purposes. In the first example, the portfolio of managers resulting from the process was sound; so were the lessons learned about life and wealth. In the second, the private equity investments would probably do fine, but the understanding of private equity, of building a business, would be extraordinary.

In fact, often forgotten in any investment strategy is that it is about more than just investment. Many years ago, I learned that the best investment advisors and stock brokers told stories. The story of Xerox, IBM, or Minnesota Mining brought investment to life and taught that investment was about creating jobs and value and world betterment. Read any year's annual report for Berkshire Hathaway and you walk away feeling that substance is taking place, business is being done, and hard work is creating jobs and value. Consider a manager looking for values in the renewable resource area, whether wind or sun or water, and how those stories can resonate with people looking forward to a long, productive life. A sound investment program reflects what we have learned about ourselves and our world. A good education program teaches us about ourselves and our world. The two go hand in hand.

A wise observer of family businesses distinguishes between the "investor" and the "owner."* Multigenerational wealth is about ownership, not merely investment. But how do we teach ownership using derivatives, passive investments, and pure quantitative analytics? How do we teach the role of our wealth in a community and the involvement of wealth holders with professional managers?

If we are looking at multigenerational wealth, we must recognize the role of investment in education. Expressed differently, we must try to connect our children and grandchildren to their wealth by allowing its investment to come across as real and productive rather than hocus-pocus magic. I will not enter the debate on whether passive investing provides more return at less cost or whether sound derivative and alternative investing can be just as secure as stocks, bonds, and real estate. But I can suggest that interesting stories and productivity provide a grounding that allows younger people (and older) to feel more comfortable and interested in their investments.

---

* Francois de Visscher, "Acting Like a Business Owner Rather than Just an Investor," *Family Business Magazine*, Spring 2010.

8

The Importance of Strategy: Capitalization

WHEN WE THINK OF THE FAMILY'S WEALTH, WE ARE USUALLY thinking of the asset side of the balance sheet. This view is too limited. Every wealth holder and every wealthy family has liabilities that should appear on the right side of the balance sheet. The obligations can be long- or short-term liabilities, they can be cash needs that must be reserved for, and they can be reflective of dreams or expectations. Managing those obligations is as much a piece of wealth management as portfolio management.

Using the traditional framework of balance sheet analytics—assets and liabilities—and talking about capitalization assists the process we need to apply wisdom on when, how, and whether to take on debt, on considerations of creating or using cash, and on whether dreams and expectations are realistic. The framework helps us answer the question "can I afford it?" under an accepted series of rules, removing the emotional involvement and introducing financial discipline. The framework also gives the wealth holder the capacity to draw on a huge pool of wisdom coming out of the world of active businesses to take into account increasingly changing assumptions about credit markets and terms of debt and values of cash.

I was visiting with a multifamily office in Dublin shortly after the Irish economy began to crumble and the former Irish wealth holders found themselves awash in debt. The CEO of the multifamily office explained: "We used to measure ourselves by clients' assets under management (AUM) but now we look at clients' debts under management (DUM)."

Defining Debt

The strategic wealth holder starts with careful definition of what should be thought of as debt. Of course, it must include any legal obligation, contractual or otherwise, such as a mortgage, credit from a bank, a tax liability, or any other legally enforceable commitment. The day a gain is realized or a taxable gift is made, a tax obligation is created and any investment decision should be made with that obligation in mind. So it is not unreasonable to reserve for taxes by creating an asset consisting of a treasury bill coming due near the date the taxes are due. This may be sound capitalization management.

But other obligations should be thought of as debt. Consider for example creating a wedding fund when you know your daughter is going to be married. It can be a savings account funded with twice the expected cost of the wedding and the understanding that whatever is left will go to charity. Once the wedding fund is set up, once you have reserved for the wedding at twice what you want it to cost, you remove worries about cost from the wedding planning process. In effect, you create a liability on the right and an appropriate asset on the left of your family financial statement.

Similarly worth considering and reserving for are your expectations with respect to tuition (even when the student to be is an infant), helping a child buy a house, vacations, and any of the other expenditures that are genuinely discretionary but that you know you will want to make.

Appropriateness of Capitalization

Business has always accepted the proposition that capital structure matters for well-run companies. The same is true of families and private wealth. In essence, families need to manage their debt, or capitalization, much like a chief financial officer in a Fortune 100 company. There must be a strategic approach to the questions of capitalization—the study of the family's assets, liabilities, net worth, and cash flow. Do the liabilities help the assets accomplish the wealth purposes? Does an examination, entity by entity—individual by individual, partnership by partnership, business by business, trust by trust—support a conclusion that each entity is sound and all entities can help move the family to its purposes?

Debt analysis is usually focused on being smart—securing good terms of interest, duration, and the like—and rarely considers being wise. Rarely is debt thought of as more than a tactical tool, a short-term arbitrage between the cost of capital and the perceived return on investment the capital supports. Most debt is sold by salespeople, primarily banks that are more interested in building a book of debt than in having it paid, more interested in the sale than the appropriateness. Most debt analytics help compare one piece of debt to another but do not encompass the suitability or sustainability of the debt.

Debt should be a strategic tool that furthers a family's economic goals whether these be the extension of economic power, the optimization of current return for a given level of risk, or financing the equity component of strategic capital expenditures. The first questions should not be whether the terms of the debt are "smart." They should be along these lines: Does the debt further the purposes of the wealth? Is it in harmony with the family's balance sheet? Is the wealth holder using the debt to make something work?

Consider the number of wealth holders who were damaged in the panic of 2008. A very smart member of a very wealthy family decided to invest in real estate. At the height of the real estate bubble, the banks were willing to throw him money at interest rates so low he could think of the money as free. Whenever he answered the phone he found a banker willing to lend him money if he would purchase more real estate. He negotiated each loan into what he considered a "smart loan," and his real estate empire grew along with his debt. His debt remained relatively small compared to a large trust of which he was a permissible beneficiary but far exceeded assets in his own name. When the real estate started to lose value and the banks began demanding more collateral, he gave freely of his assets until his entire personal wealth was collateralized and his cash flow became a trickle. It was then he looked to the trust, in his mind on his balance sheet, only to find that for 20 more years its only permissible beneficiary was charity. Indeed his capitalization was a catastrophe.

The insights we can glean from the foregoing example in terms of "capitalization theory" help us understand this wealth holder's mistakes as his assets decreased in value and his liabilities remained the same (or even increased with accruing interest). He had started with an incorrect understanding of his true balance sheet—the placement of the trust as an asset—he had incorrectly capitalized his assets (too much leverage), and he had used the wrong assets (his liquid funds) to adjust his capitalization to changing asset values. In the vernacular of lenders, he was "whipsawed" and his lender was in trouble. Potential write down by the lender put him into "workout," a process in which the bank treated him as a defaulting lender and applied pressure to collect. He was no longer a client; he was not even a customer; he was now a problem. The bank did not "treat him with the respect" he felt his "wealth" commanded. He found himself in this position because he had never built a framework of understanding to allow him to think and behave in a disciplined fashion.

A similar tragedy happened to a small family of substantial wealth. Because of a lack of process and control, the family found itself with cash needs beyond the income available and assets not easily turned into cash. It turned to borrowing to create a pool of cash that would fund cash needs for 10 years; however, that pool did not have a source of wealth to replenish it and the family's liabilities (both debt service and lifestyle) began to exceed its assets. The borrowing was not appropriate.

This story is not unique. Wealthy families all over the world overborrowed when times were good and loans cheap, and the banks had been willing participants by offering low rates, high loan-to-asset values, and imprecise documentation. When across-the-board devaluation of assets occurred in the fall of 2008, the families were left holding the bag. Few if any understood that they would have to pay the banks back, and many were stunned that their status as prominent families did not insulate them from the axe of debt collection.

Consider the global family with members in the United States and France but investment focus in the States. When that family is considering debt, what currency is appropriate? Should U.S. treasury bills be used to fund the cash needs of the French residents? How will the family reserve for obligations in France in a way that reduces currency risk? Can or should the family borrow in France or the United States to capitalize its activities? The answers will depend on the balance sheet of the family wealth enterprise.

Few wealth holders look at that balance sheet strategically with a goal of achieving the highest return on net worth. The world of private wealth is awash in smart debt. There is not much wise debt. Loans have relatively short lives with high costs of failure, whereas assets can be very long lived and have a wide range of outcomes. Although assets can both grow and shrink due to market forces, debt remains the same unless repaid, and it increases volatility of net worth for both good and bad. There are likely many families who could build a more robust and diversified balance sheet with more "wise" debt, but they will need to manage that debt with the same attention given to their assets and with a clear understanding of what the wealth is for.

Evaluating the balance sheet to determine whether and how it can help the wealth do what it is for is a complex job. Large companies have investment bankers and others skilled in financial analysis performing that job. Private wealth holders rarely have such a resource and rarely know that it is needed. The experts are frequently called in (often by the lenders) when the debt overwhelms capacity to pay; but the appropriate time to turn to experts is during the design of the family wealth management, at the beginning of the enterprise, or at least before the major decisions and commitments are made.

Starting with an understanding of what he or she is trying to accomplish with wealth, each wealth holder must consider what belongs on the right side of the balance sheet. That is, what expectations and needs should be considered beyond technical debt and legally enforceable obligations? Once an existing balance sheet is defined, managing capitalization becomes a key component of wealth management. AUM and DUM must both be considered as strategic components in making the wealth do what it is for.

9

The Importance of Strategy: Governance

THE TERM *GOVERNANCE STRUCTURE* CONJURES UP THE PENAL COL-
onies of Australia and the drudgeries of what have come to be known
as family constitutions. The words do not radiate freedom, independence, or individuality. In fact, "governance structure" is shorthand
for all of the entities and organizations that are used to manage
wealth with wisdom and process. They are wealth holders' tools to
build the relationship between themselves and their wealth. They are
the roads, the automobiles, and the traffic controls used to journey
through life without wealth burdening that journey with chaos.

Nothing requires more customization than design of these governance structures, since together they can provide individual independence or burden. Any well-designed strategy for managing
wealth will be or can lead to a governance structure that works. For
example, the foundation described in an earlier chapter, unbundled
by design and voluntarily bundled by the siblings over time, is one
such governance structure, strategically designed to accomplish set
purposes. Its evolution brought process and communication tools
to the family that ran it and a foundation for future generations to
build on. Every governance structure should be designed as well as
that one to further family goals and objectives.

Governance structures fundamentally should serve two purposes. First, they should provide the framework to ensure functionality and efficiencies as family members work together or advisors work for the wealth holder. Allowing the wealth to exist relatively unencumbered by taxes, creating the institutional operating framework for the "business of the wealth," and imposing expectations, standards, and procedures all require governance structures. Second, good governance structure is key to ensuring succession.

Succession

"Succession" is a key ingredient of legacy and multigenerational perspective. Succession requires that wealth and its efficient management pass from generation to generation and is essential for any well-run business but possibly less clearly essential for private wealth. For example, there is a sense among some trusted advisors in India that wealth works best when divided at each generation so that succession can be free floating and spawn as many successors as there are businesses.

In Canada, I was advising two brothers working in the family business with their father, a 70-year-old patriarch. The patriarch had a rule that his two sons could never fly together. That rule was reiterated over the years as one required to ensure that there would always be succession in the family business. If a plane went down with one brother on it, the other brother remained. I met with the brothers the day before the three, father and two sons, were to fly together to Moscow to visit a business partner. The brother admitted that it was unusual for the three of them to fly together, but it happened from time to time. I asked why succession was not an issue when all three flew together, and the brother said he was not sure. I was sure. Succession was the father's way of saying that in any event he wanted the company (and the support and care) of one of his sons. He did not want to be left alone if they perished together. But he would not face loneliness if all three of them met death at the same time.

Ordered succession is extraordinarily difficult to effect. Consider how many very large companies in the world struggle with succession and fail. Governance structures allow a framework to try to design the "passing of the baton." But before starting to design the structure for succession purposes, always start by asking why succession is important and what purposes it is to serve.

Succession is extremely complex when addressing an active family business. Keep in mind that portfolio wealth can always be dismantled even if that is not desirable. Even a portfolio of active businesses can be dismantled and, if needed, divided at each generation.

But many of the patriarchs of the world build a business with great care and attention and then look for succession within the family, much as Jack Welch looked for professional succession at GE. More often than not the succession planning in such cases fails.

The starting point in considering succession is to ask what the business is for. One can start with analyzing what about the family business is "family" and what is "business." How does one define *family* and how does one understand what the family should get out of the business?

A Japanese business creator whose son took over the running of the business was quite clear in his understanding of what the business was for. It was for a community of employees, and the family was to be the protector for those employees. Whether times were good or bad, the business was not to be sold because too many colleagues were dependent on the strength and values of the family.

A U.S. business creator was also clear. The business was to give the family a certain standing in the community. The business funded arts, health care, and social services through its philanthropic funds, and the creator's children and grandchildren would make all that possible through the business.

A Scandinavian patriarch had a different vision. The business was entrepreneurial and should be sold to allow all family members to enjoy the opportunity to be entrepreneurial (whether they wanted it or not).

A British family was also clear in that their business was to be a way to keep many generations wealthy—a family legacy that would ensure everyone in the family substantial wealth.

Each of these purposes has different ramifications for succession planning depending on the constituency that is to be benefited. And each has different significance with respect to governance structure, a concept related to but not necessarily synonymous with succession.

Indeed, a clear consideration is whether families' purposes are served if family members are managers, board members, or simply owners. If they are simply owners, control of the company loses significance and training in management or governance is not required. Indeed, the family members are able to live life free of the responsibility for the business but also exposed to the possibility that the business will fail in its purpose to support the family. Management and leadership might fail or, worse, take advantage of the uninvolved family members.

Purpose will also help analyze how well the business must do. If family members are to be management or board, how well must the company do to succeed in its purposes? And how expert must the family members be? If the business is to allow productive employment by family members, the bar cannot be set too high since it is always likely that family members will be worse managers than other professionals who might be available. And it is always possible that a board made up of outsiders can make for a better business than one made up of family members.

A wealth creator who decided to sell his business said: "This is about business and wealth for my family. Clearly the world will have better businessmen and better governors than even the most brilliant in my family. I created this business without any involvement of my own brothers; why do I now think my genetics will create the finest businessmen? And I would be foolish to think that the most creative and ambitious businesspeople will want to work in management or serve on the board of a business owned and run by a family. I wouldn't want that myself." He understood what the business was for and sold it for that purpose. The business was to create family wealth.

Compare that to another family business my father and I observed over three generations. The founder started a manufacturing firm in the 1930s and ran it successfully. After the Second World War, his son took over the business, and on account of careful management and a booming economy particularly benefiting that industry, the business grew dramatically. The personality of the son brought in two fine managers who, with the son, built the business into a major global business. Small ownership interests were given to those managers, and they and the son prospered. When the son's eldest son left college, the son managing the business considered the business a family business. After all, he took over from his father and wanted his son in his business as well. He let his other children pursue their passions—one son in the business was all he needed. As that son approached the age of 40, with 15 years in the business, his father decided to sell the business for a princely sum. The family would be wealthy forever more beyond its wildest expectations. Two of the three children were overjoyed, but the son who had been in the business was left without a career and without a place in life.

What happened? you ask. Essentially, the management team of son-father and his two colleagues were aging. The colleagues wanted to cash in on the fruit of their labor; the son-father determined that his own son was not of the business caliber he saw in himself. All three on the management team saw that it was time to prove to the world that they had created great value. "Selling this business makes sense for the company, the employees, and my family," the son-father said to me.

But the 40-year-old was left aimless. For him, "family business" meant his family and meant that he would have a productive way to spend his life. If that was the goal (and that would be a reasonable goal) cashing out made no sense; the family consideration would have been clear regardless of how expert he was. The father of that boy had built the expectation that the business was "for" family engagement, that its purpose was to give his 40-year-old son productive employment and involvement. Instead, after the son devoted his early career to the business, the purpose appeared to change and the business was sold.

In that case, the father subsequently funded a new business for his son. He used a small part of the proceeds from the sale of the family business, but he funded it with too little capital, too much risk aversion. The energy and risk he could put into his own business after World War II was not available to the new business. That business put his son in the hole—financially, emotionally, and in every other respect—and folded after five years.

The case is a classic one of family business succession. Too many times the creator of a family business brings his son or daughter into the business as a family business and then decides either that the son or daughter "is not up to running the business" or that it is time to prove the value created in the business. The creator has not carefully analyzed what is meant by "family business." The child is left with disappointment. The sale of the business always leaves the child perplexed and often leaves him or her feeling idle and without satisfaction.

These are not stories about governance (though governance is of course involved). These are stories about family management succession. The lesson of each is that any succession conversation must start with an understanding of what the business is for.

Tax Structuring

It is obvious that designing programs to make the wealth do what it is for requires substantial attention to the wishes and circumstances of the individuals in the family and the family as a whole. That kind of attention is not easy and the designs cannot be made uniform from family to family. On the other hand, most of the world's governance structuring is created by industries, whether financial services, accounting, or law, trying to manufacture something that can be used over and over again. Unlike human personality, which cannot easily be generalized, a jurisdiction's taxation is generalized and its management can be commoditized. For this reason, most structuring is most easily and profitably focused on taxation. However, any structuring strategy based exclusively on tax savings treats tax reduction as the purpose and goal of all wealth holders.

When wealth creators walk into my office and say they want to save taxes, I cannot design a structure until I know the answer to the question, what is the wealth for? Taxes may be what the wealth is *not* for; however, a wealth holder should strive to determine what the wealth *is* for. He or she should look for structuring strategically designed to accomplish what the wealth is for.

A classic example of structuring that does not work plays out over and over. I first ran into it in Hong Kong. The patriarch had worked with his large global accounting firm to develop the ideal structure—trusts in jurisdiction after jurisdiction, passports from the most favored countries—with taxes magnificently avoided. Taxes were avoided so long as no child or more remote descendant ever became a U.S. person, an expectation that was written into the structure. Yet the patriarch's own children went to the United States for college, fell in love with U.S. citizens, married, and had children. As the patriarch begged them all to move back to Hong Kong (for tax reasons) one after another disregarded him. Only one returned to Hong Kong with his American wife, and he became the wealth steward, but his children kept their U.S. passports.

Ten years ago, many U.S. citizens renounced their citizenship to save taxes even in the face of a statute containing draconian penalties, including treatment as a terrorist by anyone renouncing under certain circumstances. These people were pleased to be saving taxes, but their expression of accomplishment evaporated when they heard they might not be allowed to have medical attention in the United States, attend children's graduations and weddings there, or vacation in Northern California. One told me that he realized he might be a "man without a country," referring to the short story by Edward Everett Hale, a volume I gave many young Chinese people at the turn of the twenty-first century.

There is a fundamental difference between the United States and many other jurisdictions in the world, and that difference leads to considerable misunderstanding. The U.S. tax laws are fundamentally "substantial," and the tax laws of many other jurisdictions, indeed much of Europe, are "formal." This means people who think of themselves as living in London can arrange their affairs so that they are taxed elsewhere for certain purposes. They can live the life they want to live and structure their taxes among different jurisdictions.

Selecting the most desirable federal jurisdiction is not possible for the U.S. person. If the wealth inheritor of the Hong Kong patriarch wants to live in the United States, his taxes are U.S. taxes. The only recourse is to substantially avoid the United States. This is often the "tax tail wagging the dog."

In fact, if wealth is for freedom, the complex trusts and the renunciation of citizenship both fail to accomplish that goal with respect to travel and residency, at least as it involves the United States. So either freedom is lost or the structure is disregarded. That happens repeatedly when structures are designed for tax reasons. If the individual has desires for life that do not fit those structures, his or her options are to disregard structure or forego those desires.

Even without regard to tax jurisdiction, if wealth is for functionality and harmony, tax structuring can be disastrous. One of the earliest "family limited partnerships" designed for U.S. families to help avoid estate taxation was sold by a large accounting firm to a very wealthy family. The structure cleverly provided that once the family pooled all of its assets, any increase in value could pass to the children, thus avoiding the estate tax of the father. The concept made brilliant sense from a tax standpoint. The problem was that the father and his children were estranged and the children were being raised by their mother, whom the father detested. Ten years into the structure, the father was found to have removed many of the assets and the entire arrangement ended up in litigation for many years. The lawyers made money, the father and his children could never settle, and the estate lost much of its value through mismanagement during the court cases. The tax structure, a family limited partnership, required communication and harmony of a family that had neither. Indeed, the structure made harmony and functionality impossible by demanding that the family work together, trying to bundle a family that should never have been bundled.

Whenever tax-motivated strategies are deployed, a strategic consideration becomes what that strategy will do to and teach future generations. UBS was apparently selling tax fraud in the United States. Anyone using UBS for family wealth management must ask what message children and grandchildren are receiving when one's bank is using tax fraud as a marketing tool.

A parent will often hide assets, such as gold, jewelry, and even cash, to be kept secret from taxing agencies at their deaths—effectively requiring that their children and executors commit tax fraud. Do you really want criminality to be part of your family culture and a burden of stewardship to your heirs?

Structures designed for sale as "tax effective" are rarely strategic if circumstances and wealth's purposes are considered. On the other hand, structures strategically designed can be very effective in any wealth management program even in terms of saving taxes. We will consider that in more detail in the next section.

Trusts and Similar Creatures

One of the most common structuring devices in common law jurisdictions is the trust. Similar purposes can be served by corporations, limited liability companies, partnerships, and foundations in some jurisdictions. Each of these vehicles organizes management and disposition of certain assets. Each is also by its very nature limiting in that each separates the beneficiary of funds from their actual control.

Trusts and other structuring frameworks are therefore inherently controlling—sometimes called the "dead hand" guiding the wealth through generations. They are the platter from which the silent butler, the wealth steward, serves all future generations. Although duration used to be limited in almost all jurisdictions, today trusts can last forever, that is, into perpetuity in many jurisdictions. Perpetual existence is particularly popular with "dynasty thinkers" and with professional trustees enamored with the annuity-like revenue inherent in serving as trustee. But perpetuity is a long time, and I am frequently reminded of the sign on a barn in rural Missouri promoting fundamental Christianity with the question: "Eternity—where shall I spend it?"

The most successful trusts are the most flexible. The creators realize that times and people change. Expressed differently, the purpose of the wealth for me today may not be the purpose of the wealth for my children in 30 years. If the wealth is for control or protection, a trust or similar entity provides that. But flexibility is key to the success of the trust over a number of years.

Strategic design of trusts requires flexibility to be built in: power to change trustees, power to ascertain purposes and times for distribution; power in each generation to be the master of how the assets pass to their own progeny (that is, power for parents to exercise the prerogatives of parenthood); even power for each generation to make its own mistakes.

The trusts that fail almost always fail on account of rigidity. For example, 100 years ago, some U.S. trusts were written requiring all investments to be in railroad bonds. Those trusts were destined to fail with the railroads. As another example, many trusts exist without any power to change the corporate trustee even as the companies serving as corporate trustee are subsumed in other companies. How many of the dowagers naming J.P. Morgan as trustee would have imagined that their grandchildren would be at the mercy of Chemical Bank?

More subtly, so-called incentive trusts may be too rigid and serve little strategic purpose. These are trusts that attempt to control behavior by tying distributions to that behavior. For example, no distribution of funds unless the beneficiary is earning at least $100,000 in active employment; no distribution if the beneficiary marries outside the church; and no distribution until the beneficiary has children. Each of these prerequisites written into a trust assumes continuation of circumstances and values in effect at the time the trust is written. Society may change and a person's condition may change; in either event, a trustee needs the freedom to accommodate. The incentive trust is a hand deader than a doornail.

Every trust and structuring device should be approached strategically. There can be guidance in the following general rule: "He or she who does not need a trust does not mind a trust; he or she who needs a trust resents the trust." That rule applies because the well-designed trust demands appropriate management of the portfolio and expects a beneficiary to live on income or amounts not unreasonable relative to the size of the trust. The responsible person will lead his or her life reasonably with or without a trust. The spendthrift will want more than the trustees should reasonably distribute.

Selection of trustees (or similar parties) requires careful analysis and design. If you cannot find someone you trust to make the decisions you would make, you should forego the trust altogether. Look to the trustees to take all factors into account and to exercise judgment in deciding how to handle investments, how to consider distributions, and how to provide for their own succession. In other words, your trustees are responsible for seeing that the trust is managed strategically to accomplish your purposes and the purposes for its beneficiaries.

The challenge of keeping a trust fluid and dynamic is often a question of keeping the trustees dynamic. Many trusts have ancient trustees whose role as trustee becomes for them a badge of wisdom and continuing engagement. Old lawyers forced into retirement by law firms hold tenaciously to their trusteeships. A 40-year-old client resolved the problem of aging trustees by providing in his trusts that any trustee over the age of 60 years would be discharged from service. As the client aged so did the age of discharge until today the client is 85 and the age of discharge is 90.

Terms of trust distribution must be considered carefully and strategically. The age of distribution to beneficiaries really depends on purposes. If the wealth is for freedom and functionality, it might be reasonable to provide for distribution at a young age. "If my son is going to blow it," said one wise trust creator, "I'd rather he blow it young and then get on with life while he can still build a life. Otherwise, he will sit around waiting to receive the assets and then waste them after he is too old to start fresh." If the purpose of the trust is pure protection, it may not be necessary to have any automatic distribution.

There are many other strategic considerations in designing a trust. How would the creator define *incapacity* for a beneficiary or a trustee? Who should be able to remove and replace trustees? Should trustees have the power to appoint their own successors?

Expectations of appreciation in value and what is reasonable to use (whether of income or principal) enter into decisions regarding whether to provide that income is automatically distributed. In other words, a provision that the trustees must distribute income assumes that either income must somehow be a reasonable guide or investment policy should follow determination of a beneficiary's need. A requirement of income distribution may discourage the trustee from pursuing strategies of capital appreciation.

All of these considerations enter into the terms of trusts and other structuring devices and should never be seen as boilerplate. Yet, for most trust creators, these and other details are simply resolved in a "standard form" of trust.

Trusts and other structuring devices can offer strategic opportunities. These include the many tax reduction opportunities so often promoted by banks, lawyers, and accountants. But there are others. In the 1970s my father and I redesigned a trust that Congress thought it had eliminated and that combined charity and private beneficiaries in a way that looked good from a tax standpoint. It was called a charitable lead trust, and, as we recommended these trusts to some of our clients, we sought and received the first five or six rulings from the Internal Revenue Service holding that the trusts were effective and not subject to tax challenge. In several of those cases, the wealth holders, each a wealth creator, expressed contempt for charity but agreed to establish the trust as a way to take money away from the U.S. government even if some went to charity. In each of those cases, the trust turned the creator and, more importantly, his family into philanthropists because in each case the family came to realize the strategic benefit of relating to community through philanthropy. One of the creators had never given a cent to charity. Today his widow and family have given not only from the trust but tens of millions of dollars beyond those amounts.

We have also used charitable lead trusts strategically to teach younger family members. One was set up several years ago for three children who were named trustees and directed to manage investments and choose charitable beneficiaries each year. The investment strategy was complicated, as the trust required an annual charitable gift well beyond its income. So the trustees had to design a reserve to meet that requirement over five years rather than relying on increasing markets. Implementing that strategy required discussion, understanding, and education relating to issues of volatility, liquidity, and cash retention. Selection of the charities was casual in the first two years and proved unsatisfying, as the children found little accountability by the donees. Within three years, the children were developing processes and communications to elicit grants and to require regular reports. In effect, the trust itself taught investment principles and allowed a relatively comfortable development of collaborative process. The three children learned and worked together in a disciplined fashion. Once again we have found these trusts could play a strategic role in the management of the family wealth.

Estate Planning

Estate planning is the process of determining gifts and divisions of property and of designing the structures to be used during lifetime and at death. Trusts and other structuring entities are the tools of estate planning. Often, these tools are used before the framework is ready; the carpenter is hammering nails before the architect creates the building plan. Designing the structure requires strategic consideration first.

Consider a most unstrategic estate plan—that of King Lear. He planned to die with nothing, but he left himself nothing to live on and threw his daughters into dysfunctional chaos. His plan was conceived less for estate tax than for dynastic succession, but under the U.S. estate tax regime, the ideal estate tax plan remains Lear's— to die with nothing owned and nothing taxed. Yet, how strategic is that? Just like Lear, clients are being urged to make gifts of their residence ("you can always lease it back from your children"), to create trusts that end up leaving them penniless, and to bundle themselves irrevocably with their children, who somehow end up with control.

Strategic consideration of any estate plan can start with several principles. First and foremost, consider what the wealth is for and whether and to what extent you want to retain the unilateral power to consume or use it. You must answer important questions before a tax plan is developed. You cannot answer those questions without some sense of what you are trying to accomplish. What do you want to retain? What value, if any, do you want your children to have? What strategic benefit do you want to derive from charitable gifts?

The ideal estate plan reduces the value of property in the hands of the older generation in a way that increases the value of property in the hands of the younger generation. Great opportunities lie in making gifts and even paying gift taxes. Charitable and private gifts allow tax benefits because they can effect reduction of value in parents and increase of value in children.

Reducing the value of parents' assets and increasing the value in the hands of their children can be illustrated with an interesting example. There are two copies of a rare book, both owned by a father. Each is worth $50,000. The father gives one copy to his son. When he burns the other, the value of the property in the hands of his son becomes $75,000. If burning a book offends you, give the book to a rare book library, which effectively destroys its market and takes it out of commerce with the same effect as burning it. In either case, the reduction of value in the wealth holder's asset directly increases that of the child's.

Estate planning is frequently complicated by collections of tangible property, by real estate, and by property otherwise laden with sentiment. Collectors must ask what their collections are for. If a collection is for legacy and not monetary investment, does it make sense to leave it to the children? In the United States, if collectors leave their collections to their children and an estate tax is levied, the children must pay in taxes an amount equal to the collection's value—in effect they have to buy it from the collector for its value. Collectors who make their children "buy" the collection are also changing the character of the owners. Whereas the original owners were the collectors, their children become the curators.

What the collection is for effectively solves the problem of turning the "collector" family into the "curator" family. If the collection is an investment, it should be sold. If the collection is a legacy, it should be given to a museum.

Family retreats and family vacation property need to be evaluated similarly. These pieces of property often become divided generation after generation ultimately held by a number of people, some of whom bear the costs and some of whom do not. Dividing the ownership of the property among many people frequently causes friction and unhappiness. Again, the solution becomes obvious when the purposes are set out. If it is investment property, it should be sold. If it is sentimental property, it should be given to a public agency or a charity.

As we can see, strategic estate planning starts with the question of what the individual is trying to accomplish. All plans must further that purpose; and special assets, whether collections or sentimental property, must be taken into account as investments or otherwise.

Dispositions at Death

If estate planning is seen as all about designing lifetime giving to accomplish tax purposes, we can lose sight of an important consideration—where one's wealth should go at death.

Laws of intestacy are enacted to establish where property should go if there is no other direction. Few substantial wealth holders die "intestate," that is, without a will. But before a wealth holder can shake off intestacy, he or she must examine the purpose of the wealth.

We are talking about "family wealth." That means it is owned by people who are private parties and somehow are connected to family. Wealth can be "owned" by different members of a family, but it cannot be owned by an entire family as if by one person. A Chinese patriarch once tried to explain that in China, wealth ownership is thought of differently from other places. Wealth, he said, is thought of as owned by the family and not by any individual. Yet notwithstanding that statement, I pointed out that Chinese law has developed trusts for estate disposition allowing an "owner" to decide whether to leave the wealth to family, mistress, or charity. Consider again that individual family members cannot have economic benefit from the full pot of the family wealth, and control cannot be exercised unilaterally by every family member except by excluding every other member. If a table has one pie, each of four diners cannot have all of it. So with family wealth. Somehow members of a family must share it; and if we talk about wealth owned by a family, we necessarily must contemplate some sharing of that wealth.

Family wealth need not be irrevocably for family, though most jurisdictions in the world have some requirement that at least part of a person's wealth be left to a spouse. However, most wealth holders leave their wealth to spouse and children, as much as a "default" disposition as on account of fondness and affection. If part of what the wealth is for requires an analysis of how much is enough and how much is too much, disposition to charity becomes integral. Trusts can be to deprive children of benefits as much as for protection. A spouse's interest must be considered in terms of his or her capacity to control the wealth during life and at death. Can the wealth pass to a subsequent spouse? Can the widow or widower decide to treat children differently? All of these issues require careful consideration and strategic analysis.

We all say we want to treat our children or grandchildren "equally" as if the definition is somehow clear when in fact definitions of equality require careful analysis. The common definition seems to be dollar-for-dollar equality—when my son gets a dollar, my daughter gets a dollar. Another definition may be that needs are met equally. While the wealth holder is alive, he or she may pay tuition for one child without equalizing by giving the other the same amount to spend on a luxury car. Should this change at death? Suppose one child has built huge independent wealth and the other has pursued a career as a teacher. Should each receive the same dollar amount?

How do we define equality in gifts to grandchildren when one child has two children and one child has four? Do grandchildren by one child share half as one-quarter each and the other share half as one-eighth each? Or are assets for grandchildren divided equally with an equal share for each grandchild? This is sometimes described as per capita as opposed to per stirpes division. I often find that per capita division for each grandchild becomes more prevalent as the donor comes to know the grandchildren as individuals—and this is because any purpose of wealth must focus on its use by individuals rather than the stock of ancestry.

The questions that must be answered when writing a will or providing for gifts during life are numerous. Each can be answered in isolation from the others, but sound planning for disposition requires harmonization of all the answers. The harmonization follows only when there is a grounded strategy for accomplishing the articulated purposes, an understanding of the role of wealth in the family and among one's loved ones.

Family Office

A well-run family office can be the temple for the family wealth, where the high priests gather wisdom and follow process to allow everyone to have the blessings of the wealth. A poorly designed family office can actually keep the wealth from doing what it is supposed to do and can become a dark dungeon enslaving the family and all of its members in dysfunction and without wisdom. Careful strategic consideration must go into whether to have a family office and how to design it. Most family offices evolve out of a business or a close relationship between a patriarch and accountant, bookkeeper, or employee of the active business. Systems and operations evolve often without careful thought other than how to build efficiencies. The office grows "organically," without much attention to purposes or strategy until processes and relationships are in place and relatively stagnant. By the time the family or a family member wants to consider whether and how the office should work, employees, systems, and "ways of doing things" are often fossilized; infrastructure, administration, and management are not easy to change.

Even if change is possible, family offices are complex, and there are no models that fit all. Instead, someone must sift through best practices, attend sessions and courses on the topic, and hire consultants to help fix or create the family office. The easy fixes are efficiencies; the hard fixes are making the family office meet the family's needs. Until the development of the Standards of Private Wealth Management, there were no easy systems or processes or even ways to build them strategically. Clearly, building a functioning family office through creation or remodeling is very difficult and requires substantial effort.

If one purpose of the wealth is to allow self-actualization—freedom to be all a person can be—it is difficult for a single-family office to further wealth's purposes. Creation or remodeling is difficult and time consuming. Even the well-designed and -operated single-family office requires some involvement by family members—as a steward, as a board, or as participants in some other way. Often a family member is designated to run the office, and he or she is then burdened with managing the wealth of the family (with or without compensation).

Within several months of Bernie Madoff's exposure, I ran into the artist who had attended my talk on freedom from wealth (see Chapter 2). She had achieved "freedom from wealth," she said, and that had made her happy. But after the events of 2008 she was unhappy again. The spread of distrust had touched her and her family office. I told her I could guess why she was unhappy. She was spending time again in the family office as she and her cousins wondered whether they could trust those running the family office, feeling that they needed to be more engaged in the office. Despite the woman's decision that she would lead a life of freedom from wealth, the dynamics of the family office and the circumstances of the financial crisis had combined to throw her into administration, governance, and attention to detail at the office. Her freedom was curtailed.

With trust shaken, the artist felt she had no recourse other than micromanagement. As we discuss later, wealth management standards, easily set and assessed, would have allowed her the systems and processes needed to restore her freedom.

We see the difficulties inherent in a family office structure when a family starts to consider the relatively innocuous decision of where to locate the family office when family members live everywhere. Is the location near the patriarch or matriarch? Or, in one case I know, in the city where the trusted advisor to the patriarch chooses to live but far from all members of the family? What is the strategic message sent to the family with respect to control and accountability? When the patriarch of that family dies, the family office may exist for the convenience of the advisor.

Recall the 90-year-old family office executive who called the 60-year-olds "boys and girls" and one of whose "girls" felt like a bird freed from a cage when the office closed. That superannuated executive ran the office as his fiefdom and for the benefit of himself and his staff. The family members were merely cogs in the mechanism of "running an office." Family offices can take on a life of their own, and family members can become irrelevant. It is challenging for any family to keep this from happening.

Compensation is always a difficult aspect of running a family office. Are family members compensated for their efforts, and if so, what is expected of them? Is this a way of forcing the shackles of stewardship on a family member, and is that fair to that person? How can the employees of a family be compensated so they are clearly sitting on "the family's side of the table." Surely, short-term profits should not be the standard. And it may be that investment performance should be seen as completely irrelevant, particularly if the family is relying on "industrial-strength" management.

But the question requiring most strategic analysis is exactly what is wanted in a family office. Fundamentally, "family office" is the tool for making the wealth do what it is for. There are large family foundations that are in fact family offices because the administration of philanthropy allows for all the purposes of the family wealth by building processes and communication to allow the family to work together and with its community. For other families, an investment-only house is the best family office. The reason is not necessarily because investment return is the ultimate goal of the wealth, but because the family has decided that each member should have complete independence while sharing the infrastructure and cost of money management. And some family offices have only "concierge services" because in that way, their individual needs can be best met with respect to those matters least easily commoditized.

In fact, the ideal family office has many of the following features:

* It is professionally run, possibly building in the efficiencies available when a number of families share professional management and ownership.
* It has a clear plan for succession of management, insulating family as much as possible from the challenges of replacing departing staff.
* It allows the family to set policy and detail by articulating what it wants of its wealth without requiring the family to manage policy, detail, or implementation.
* It recognizes that the individual is paramount and that the needs of each individual must be met in a customized fashion.
* It can be neutral in judgment with respect to individual needs so that it can serve the needs of many generations, many jurisdictions, and many cultures.
* It accesses "industrial-strength" due diligence but understands and meets individual investment needs.
* It is unconflicted in every respect, and its employees are incentivized by success in helping the wealth achieve its purposes.

If those are the features of the ideal family office, that ideal is almost impossible to find and extraordinarily difficult for any family to build. That it is difficult to build, however, should not keep a family from trying. Any attempt to build or find such an ideal family office should start with an understanding of what the family is trying to accomplish. Then it should progress with strategic analysis of how to build wisdom and process to permeate everything the office does and every service it provides, with the entire structure designed to give each family member freedom and independence.*

---

* Regulations adopted by the U.S. Securities and Exchange Commission in June 2011 may pose significant challenges to any single family office desiring to offer freedom in an environment of privacy. These regulations must now be considered by any family with its own family office or by those planning on building one.

The Importance of Strategy: Family Legacy and Values

"FAMILY LEGACY AND VALUES" SOUNDS ELOQUENT, AND THE PHRASE has become the clarion opening of many family wealth conversations. "Legacy" takes us together as a family through history, and "values" bind us forevermore. Those words give perpetuity to the family just as trusts now give perpetuity to the wealth.

But though the words roll out with grandeur, the pragmatics of designing family legacy and embracing family values are difficult. Indeed the road to functionality is strewn with the carcasses of legacies and values.

Legacy and values require very careful consideration by any individual or family that has made a decision to articulate and perpetuate them. There are issues of process—are they announced by a patriarch or matriarch or developed collaboratively? There are issues of history—how were they found in the family's story and how can they be incorporated into the family story? And there are issues of placement—where do they belong so they become part of the personality of every family member?

The best place to start in designing, articulating, and implementing family legacy and values is in strategy. If the purposes are to hold the family together (to keep it bundled on some level), to ensure that

95

the family members will forever feel responsible to each other and their community, and to build a strong sense of identity, the strategic question to ask is what will work.

The key to answering that question is that what can work must be genuine and must be capable of surviving many generations, many jurisdictions, and many cultures. With those requirements, it should be clear that few "legacy and values" programs can really work. The pitfalls are obvious. First comes the assumption that the family can make its legacy worthy of admiration, particularly when wealth creators and many wealth inheritors are not entirely savory characters. We have already seen how legacy and family name can be beatified through philanthropy, but that goes only partway. Consider the divorces, the dalliances, the personal and moral failures certain to hit every family over its generations. How many families in the United States are without the horse thief in their legacy? How many European families include more than one war criminal?

More significantly, shared legacy necessarily leaves out the in-laws, each of whom becomes a central character in his or her nuclear family and beyond. Consider the Daughter of the American Revolution, the descendant of slave owners, who marries the African American descendant of slaves. How do they talk to their children about family legacy?

And if shared legacy becomes exclusionary (as it must), shared values can become a kind of polite code for disapproval of other cultures and other values. One German family I know says that their values are classic Teutonic values. When the family office head is asked what happens if a marriage is multicultural, he says, "That will not happen; we do not approve." How will the woman from New Delhi marrying into the family feel about those Teutonic values?

Let's look at other ways values can be exclusionary:

- A Jewish woman marries into a Christian family that holds family business meetings on Saturday.
- A Muslim man marries into a Chinese family unwilling to invest according to Sharia law.
- A family defines the family's values as part of its constitution but refuses to include in-laws in those discussions. More than one of those in-laws feels like an outsider because of the "values" as they are defined by that family.

♦ A Scandinavian family decides that family legacy and family values are embodied in entrepreneurialism and designs the entire wealth management program around that. That looks fine until it is recognized that not every human is designed to build for profit. There are artists, musicians, doctors, lawyers, and others. Are they excluded from that family or simply at odds with the legacy and values?

What is the harm of values that are exclusionary? If values are to be an ingredient of legacy and legacy is to be perpetual and families are always expanding as in-laws join and children are related by blood to in-laws, exclusionary values will fail as the bedrock of legacy.

Strategic design of family values must work to serve as a foundation for legacy. First, the values should be as flexible as possible and should not be yet another action of the "dead hand." Just as railroad bonds destroyed more than one trust, white supremacy or anti-Semitism can destroy a family's harmony. Certain values are as out of date as the gold standard, and no legacy and values exercise can foresee the developments of perpetuity. Indeed, a family might conclude that the only family value certain to survive unscathed and unscathing would be the value of inclusion. If their wealth is for functionality and harmony and individuality and freedom, perhaps they incorporate no more than inclusion in their value statement. There may be certain universal and fundamental principles that should be observed—the Golden Rule comes to mind. But are those really appropriately in a family values statement or do they belong under human values?

> Our family legacy is one of tolerance. We tolerate all family members regardless of their flaws and peccadilloes, and we welcome them wherever they come from and whatever they do. Our family values are to be loving and inclusive of anyone who enters our family at any time.

To whom is this attributed? It's a great paragraph; it's just floating, without copyright and available to anyone. Any family should feel free to use it as family legacy and family values and then move on to other matters.

The Importance of Strategy: Next Generation Education

INCREASINGLY, NEXT GENERATION EDUCATION IS BEING OFFERED for wealthy children. Like students at Sunday school, high school students attend weekend courses put on by associations, banks, and other financial service companies to educate them in wealth. Parents pack their children off to "wealth schools" to learn how to balance checkbooks and understand the intricacies of risk and performance. A bank builds a social networking platform for children of ultra-high-net-worth clients to allow those children to easily associate with other wealthy inheritors to be.

What strategies do these serve? Many people in the world learn to keep a checkbook, file tax returns, and run their accounts without recourse to special lessons. Most people cannot afford to hire staff to run their finances, but they muddle through somehow. Many wealth holders are happy to be friends with people of more limited wealth. And many people lead happy lives even if they cannot serve as their own financial advisor. Education in finance may be helpful, but "exclusive" courses limited to children of wealth do not help those children adapt to real life. In fact, those courses may unnecessarily isolate them from the rest of the world.

If functionality is the goal, it will occur most naturally when people feel they have control over their lives and the freedom to engage fully in the excitement and challenge of living. Being schooled on Saturday as a "rich child" surrounded only by other rich children really furthers no aspiration or independence or joy of living in a world.

What goals should be met through education of the next generation? What should matter to these wealth inheritors is how connected they feel to their families and communities, how free they are to choose their own associations on their own terms, and how fully they can engage in interests and pursuits that keep them productive through their lives. With careful planning by their parents and grandparents, these wealth inheritors can have good investment managers, family office staff, and others to manage their affairs and to give them the freedom they need to lead life. Whether their portfolios increase at 10 percent or 20 percent is not really likely to be decisive to their happiness. Why focus education on how to hire investment managers and family office staff? Why not look for ways to help them become all they can be without the limitation of being categorized as "rich"? If the next generation must be trained in money matters, careful effort might be made not to leave them feeling isolated from their friends and those with whom they might otherwise associate.

Next generation education needs to be designed strategically, starting with the question, "What do I really want my children to learn and how do I want them to learn it? How do I want them to lead their lives?" The curriculum for that usually starts with love and attention.

I have seen strategically designed programs where grandparents regularly engage their grandchildren in philanthropy. One involves an annual weekend where the grandparents and grandchildren meet in their grandparents' hometown. The grandparents set a fund amount for disposition, and they and the grandchildren meet with various charities and visit various programs all selected by the grandchildren and grandparents in the months before the weekend. Together, the grandparents and grandchildren review and analyze what they have seen and assign to each grandchild a report to the group to be prepared during the month after the weekend. After reviewing those reports and during a conference call set up for the purpose, the allocated funds are divided among the selected charities and any letters of condition are prepared for transmittal with the gift.

How much fine education comes from that exercise? First, there is a sense of legacy and community inherent in the collaborative effort to help a community. Second, there is a sense of finance and numbers as the grandchildren work through divisions to meet the needs of each charity. Third, the exercise teaches process and discipline. All of these lessons come wrapped in love, family, and community and are effective because of that.

The most successful next generation education about wealth management comes through the model parents and grandparents can offer and through personal experiences handled one-on-one. We have seen that investment programs can be educational. So any other element of a wealth management program should be seen as most effective if learning goes with it.

Opportunities for teaching children abound:

+ A request for money to buy a house can lead to learning if, for example, the details of considering a mortgage are used strategically to develop cash-flow understanding and budgeting. An inheritor's question—whether to buy outright or take out a mortgage—can be used for an extensive interactive session to answer the question in terms of the inheritor's cash flow, cash needs, principal, and similar elements.
+ What better way to teach about risk than to have a conversation with a young person who has been solicited by a life insurance agent?
+ How better to introduce fundamental concepts of estate planning than to enter a detailed discussion with new parents about what should happen to their young child if both of them die before the child is an adult?
+ How better to build an understanding of the family office than to have the family office build a substantial process and series of sessions for an individual family member around his or her first simple question?
+ Trusts and other structures can be designed in part to educate as previously discussed.

* What better way to introduce philanthropy than to spend considerable time and attention considering the first charitable gift a young person mentions?

Utilizing elements of the wealth management program for education, one-on-one and as the child is ready, is the most strategic way to accomplish any goal of family wealth. If those opportunities provided by the wealth management program are difficult for the parent to use as tools for education (and they often are), they are perfectly designed to be used by a trusted advisor and, in some cases such as philanthropy, by a grandparent. But each opportunity carefully and strategically designed to be used as a tool with goals in mind can work to achieve those goals.

However, although any element of the wealth management program can be used to teach what needs to be taught about wealth management, the wisest wealth holders recognize that the most important lesson is in love and self-confidence and learning to be all you can be. Taking a family vacation, coaching a soccer team, attending a school play, or reading a bedtime story are much more effective tools to educate a child in life and love than any formal education program. Without hiding the fact that the family has money, the message can be conveyed that money is by its nature minor in definition of self and family.

Love, attention, and caring communicate the importance of life, freedom, and self better than any Saturday class at the bank.

12

The Role of Wealth Management Standards

WISDOM AND PROCESS ARE THE FOUNDATIONS OF SOUND WEALTH management. The strategies that are implemented must allow the harmonization of all elements of the wealth management operation—from investments to philanthropy to governance to education and well beyond.

Wisdom starts with the understanding of what the wealth is for; until that understanding is developed, there can be no strategy that works. The purpose of the wealth must be articulated individual by individual and may change from time to time. Deciding what the wealth is for and ensuring that it is current is the responsibility of the wealth holder and cannot be delegated. The wealth holder can look to a trusted advisor for help, but ultimately he or she bears the burden of setting out the vision.

Building strategies and following processes, executing the vision of what wealth is for, requires expertise that many wealth holders do not have as well as considerable time and attention that many wealth holders do not want to devote. The management of significant family wealth, like any worthwhile enterprise, requires standards to govern operations, to measure performance, to ensure proper process, and ultimately to avoid disasters like Madoff, Stanford, and others. A wealth holder wanting to live life free from the burdens of wealth will want to delegate the management of wealth but will require accountability and measurement tools to ensure that the wealth is being managed appropriately.

The organization of large companies can provide guidance. In large companies, a board of directors sets direction and vision, while employees with expert skills work under complex organizational structures to accomplish those purposes. Leadership, business plans, strategies, and many employees make it all work. Processes are in place to assure appropriate execution of the business strategy, succession plans, responsiveness to various constituencies, and adherence to standards set internally or externally. Regular reviews and audits assure the board that proper actions are being taken and that they have what they need to know that the company is being properly operated.

The wealth holder or, when the family is working together, the family is in effect the board of directors and delegates management to others. Few wealth holders have much apparatus for managing portfolio wealth. Few, if any, family offices operate with the infrastructure of a Fortune 500 company. In fact, given the limitations on any family office, it will be difficult to design such infrastructure.

Good corporate CEOs consider planning their succession as one of their highest priorities. Family offices rarely think about succession until the vacancy occurs. In Switzerland, I visited the office of a family with huge wealth. I met with the three employees heading up the operations, and one said to me with pride that the three of them, all in their 60s, had more than 90 years' experience with the family. I marveled at that loyalty and then asked simply what succession plans they had for themselves. They had none.

The board of a well-run company always has its expectations for job performance articulated and its review procedures well developed. Worldwide, family office executives bemoan the fact that their "constituents" do not appreciate how well they do their jobs. Of course, some constituents actually do understand the efforts and skill it takes, but not all. And more than one family office executive has taken advantage of his or her position to defraud the family.

"How can wisdom and process be institutionalized in family wealth to become part of the family office's DNA?" asked one British family office executive. The DNA of most families is not process-oriented; as previously discussed, the de facto boardroom table is the dining room table where father and mother govern through authority and not process.

So how can the family wealth management system have clear rules for articulating purpose, for ensuring that proper roles are played, for setting out proper investment procedure, for requiring succession planning, and for protecting against dishonesty and fraud? The answer lies in standards. Industry after industry has developed objective, universal standards for operation to ensure that owners, management, and customers have a process to make certain that business is well run.

All of the following rely on or represent standards consistently applied:

+ A corporate audit
+ A commercial flight from Los Angeles to Sydney
+ An ATM in Shanghai accessed with a debit card from a U.S. bank
+ The USB port found in almost any computer
+ Time zones
+ Weights and measures used in business and commerce

Most of the world's great businesses have internal standards that allow them to manufacture the same product to the same specifications whether in Shanghai or St. Louis. Ford Motor Company became a global company by requiring standards of all its suppliers. FedEx and other delivery companies set standards on which its staff and customers can rely worldwide.

Service providers in the financial services industry are usually subject to standards. There are regulatory frameworks, fiduciary or suitability requirements, governing the management of investment decisions for pension plans, superannuation funds, foundations, endowments, insurance reserves, and personal trusts. Surprisingly, there are few such standards for the management of private wealth, particularly global private wealth. The regulatory framework is jurisdictional and complex so that there is no single standard or imposed framework for wealth that is managed across a number of jurisdictions. A fiduciary standard becomes confusing in a jurisdiction without common-law trusts. Without a common standard or framework there also can be no commonly accepted auditing or review processes for family wealth management.

The Development of Principles and Standards

The concern that process must be clear and must start with some understanding of what it is trying to accomplish led to the promulgation of the Principles of Private Wealth Management by the Lowenhaupt Global Advisors' Global Council in January 2009. Those Principles have become the basis of an international initiative sponsored by the Institute for Wealth Management Standards, a not-for-profit Swiss entity, to develop standards based on those Principles—the creation of Principles-based Standards.

The Principles evolved shortly after the Madoff Ponzi scheme was uncovered and the world had watched Bear Stearns, AIG, Lehman, and others fall into oblivion. It was clear to many of us that wealth holders needed protection and that governments and regulators were not likely to provide it.

The Madoff scandal was announced on a Thursday night, December 11, 2008. By chance, I had breakfast the next morning with a person who had run a large family office in New York. She was to take me to meet a well-known and highly respected estate planning attorney in New York. When I asked her whether she had heard of Bernard Madoff, she replied: "Bernie, of course, why?" I showed her the *New York Times* and she turned pale. She told me that the family she had worked for had invested 100 percent of its liquidity, more than $1.2 billion, with Bernie. "I told them not to trust him with all their money," she said.

We met the attorney at his office, where tension was visible in the activity of its lawyers. The attorney opened our visit by saying that he represented seven families that were "billionaires yesterday and broke today—Madoff victims." He served on several foundations that had all their money placed in Madoff. "We all thought Bernie had integrity and we trusted him," the attorney said.

This analysis was troubling. It is not sound to rely exclusively on integrity and trust. Any good swindler starts by building the reputation for integrity—without that, he or she could not be a successful swindler. And trust is subjective; I can trust someone whom others do not trust. Telling someone not to trust Bernie is like telling me not to love my wife—neither has an objective, disciplined analysis available.

Clearly, integrity and trust are the beginning points of a process, and there is no need to undertake the process unless you believe the advisor has integrity and is trustworthy. But after concluding that an advisor can be trusted, wealth holders need to adhere to certain Principles that allow them to say: "I love you and I trust you, but I cannot use you because you do not allow me to comply with my principles, which are objective and immutable."

The Madoff fraud inspired the conversation at Lowenhaupt Global Advisors' Global Council and many other exchanges with wealth holders, family office executives, and professional advisors. These conversations resulted in 15 Principles to be considered by any private wealth holder in managing wealth.

The Principles are fundamental, not best practices. They are not ideals. Instead they are simple and straightforward, and they are not likely to be seen as controversial. The Principles are intended to cover all areas of a person's relationship to his or her wealth to allow the harmonization and the development of strategies to accomplish specific, well-defined purposes. They are principles and not rules, so they can be selected, modified, and adjusted individual by individual and family by family. But first and foremost, they are the guiding principles and lay down a foundation of process-driven wealth management.

A key benefit of the Principles is that they give families an opportunity to build process into wealth management and decide which of the Principles should be adopted. A Chinese patriarch said to me about the Principles: "This is the ideal way to sit down with my children and grandchildren to talk about the overarching principles of managing wealth for generations to come without our spending time on details." In this way, the Principles themselves become a teaching tool.

The Principles include articulating what the wealth is for, setting clear and reasonable governance structures, adhering to sound fiduciary practices, considering succession, prohibiting self-dealing, defining reasonable compensation systems for employees, and considering the fundamentals of custody, transparency, and comprehension of strategies. Requiring separation of management and custody and auditing, insisting on transparency, asking that someone not aligned with the wealth holder evaluate and understand any investment strategy, and insisting on clear and careful monitoring would all have kept the wealth holder away from Madoff. Thorough diversification would have avoided much of the damage wreaked by Madoff, Stanford, Lehman, AIG, and the other terrors of 2008.

Based on the collective analysis from the Global Council and others with long experience in managing significant wealth, we would have told Madoff this:

> Bernie, although we trust you and believe you have the highest integrity, we cannot use you because you do not separate custody and management and you do not have independent accountants. My people cannot understand why your strategy works. I'd like to use you, but I cannot. If I find a pair of shoes that is good looking and I would love to own, but they are size 8 and I am size 11, I cannot buy them. The same goes for you.

Bernie did not fit the wealth holder adopting the Principles.

Principles are hard to build into a family's DNA. They reflect wisdom, but they cannot be absorbed as process. Good principles can, in theory, encourage safe flights or safe operation of electronics, for example. But standards are required to allow many people engaged in one flight's safety to collaborate to create safety in practice. An electrical outlet is effectively theory brought to practice through international standards. Indeed, much of the operation of our world works because of global standards.

The mission of the Institute for Wealth Management Standards is to build global principles-based standards. Those Standards are now being reviewed and considered by wealth holders worldwide and are being incorporated into the DNA of many families of significant wealth. Details and how they will work are among the subjects of Part 2.

With defined Principles and Standards, providers of investment, legal, and accounting advice will have clear articulation of the requirements to be imposed on them. To make true progress in the

---

SOAP BOX

As we have witnessed repeatedly for the past two decades, securities regulations do not fully protect wealth holders. In fact, there is growing evidence that there is an inverse relationship between regulations and instances of abuse and fraud.

Complicated disclosures make it more difficult for the wealth holder to make informed investment decisions, and voluminous regulations only make it easier for dishonest advisors to hide within the system.

The fact that Bernie Madoff was registered with the U.S. Securities and Exchange Commission (SEC) no doubt lulled wealth holders around the world into thinking that the SEC had conducted its own due diligence on Bernie, and there was no need for the wealth holder to replicate the effort.

---

way private wealth is managed, families need to challenge their providers to behave in a way that complies with the Standards. As one wealth holder put it: "If a billion-dollar family goes to JP Morgan and says it wants transparency of fees and assets, JP Morgan can disregard the family and find many other billion-dollar families. But if 200 families of that size demand transparency of Morgan, Morgan will accede to the demand." In fact, the Standards will bring bulk to the demands of private wealth holders and change how providers serve their clients by giving families a common vocabulary and position. A platform and forum will evolve for communication of demands and expectations.

With principles-based standards, family members will no longer need to micromanage their wealth. Trust is no longer the sole standard. Our artist, who went back into the family office after 2008, can instead serve on a board of directors knowing that process is in place, capable of audit and capable of certification. Other families will be relieved of the obligation and stewardship to create their own rules of operation and can instead rely on these Principles and Standards.

13

The Transition from Reflections to Implementation

SOUND WEALTH MANAGEMENT—HARMONIZING WEALTH AND life—requires wisdom and process: wisdom to know what you want to accomplish and what the wealth is for, and process to allow objective management of those goals and objectives. Sound process removes family dynamics, allows delegation of responsibilities, and gives every family member both the comfort of knowing that affairs are being managed and the freedom to live his or her life to its fullest.

Yet, the statement that sound wealth management requires wisdom and process leaves heads nodding and minds wondering, "How do we do that?" Wisdom is not easy to find. The world's largest companies have employees, boards of directors, and consultants all trying to provide wisdom. How does an individual or family access that wisdom? One must build wisdom if it is to inform all decisions, and building wisdom requires a grounding of understanding of one's self and one's own goals and aspirations.

Sound process is never easy to build. Like a house, it must be built in interlocking details by professionals rather than by those who live in it. It is nearly impossible for a wealth holder to build harmonizing processes—processes that further the purposes of wealth across every

111

aspect of life and over many generations. The wealth holder can buy advice in many areas and can read books that provide many details of explanation. But how does the wealth holder find help putting together a family wealth management program that can be run by others and monitored and assessed independently?

The answer seems clear, but until now no one had developed the resource. Each wealth holder should adopt principles that all who are servicing the wealth holder must follow. Those principles require conversations and decisions that make clear what the wealth is for and on what basis, generally, it is to be managed to accomplish those purposes. The principles are those of the wealth holder and not of the service providers; the service providers are to abide by the wealth holder's principles.

Once the wealth holder or family develops the principles, their implementation can be accomplished by standards and a business plan that allows all of those involved to know the rules, clearly and uniquely set out to support the principles. The standards need to be developed by independent and objective professionals who have the capacity and training to set out the management of each principle. Tools and resources can then be allocated to ensure that select service providers can do their jobs efficiently and effectively. Once the business plan is created, it can be monitored, assessed, and modified over time, and professionals running the family wealth can be evaluated objectively by the wealth holder or others.

Today each wealth holder, family, or family office is an island independently struggling to gather wisdom and process. The islands are surrounded by a sea of service providers who have developed systems and processes (generally compliant with governing law) to serve not only customers but also the employees and owners of the service providers. The goal here is to help wealth holders design *their* own unique processes to accomplish *their* own purposes.

The Framework Associated with a Wealth Management Ethos

Going from principles to standards requires a framework to guide an informed, evaluative process. How do we place this development, how do we ground the construction, in a proven foundation that can be easily recognized as valid and tested by the industry and easily engaged by the wealth holder?

We have no law governing what the wealth holder must do. Instead we must look to identify a framework that can bind the wealth holder's principles to defined private wealth management standards—a framework that is based on common concepts and a vocabulary that can be easily understood by the wealth holder and service providers alike.

This volume has adopted just such a framework in Ethos. Ethos as developed by 3ethos under the leadership of Don Trone is now being used by a number of companies and individuals in the financial services industry. Its method and vocabulary are easily understood, and it is an excellent tool for analysis that provides easy communication of principles-based standards by private wealth holders.

Ethos is based on a five-step decision-making process: analyze, strategize, formalize, implement, and monitor:

1. **Analyze** allows us to focus on the fundamental principle that each wealth holder is responsible for articulating his or her own goals and objectives—"What is the wealth for?" It also requires that our program identify the persons who will be responsible for managing the wealth management program and the rules, regulations, and trust provisions that will impact the wealth management process.

2. **Strategize** is focused on the critical factors that must be considered by decision makers when developing the wealth holder's strategy—the wealth holder's sources and levels of risk; assets and asset class preferences; time horizons; and short-to-intermediate-term performance objectives.

3. **Formalize** requires that decision makers develop a formal business plan that outlines how the overall wealth management program will be executed.

4. **Implement** takes us from strategy to implementation—specifically, how experts are going to be selected to implement the strategy defined in Step 3.

5. **Monitor** reminds us that the best plans are worthless unless they are regularly reviewed to determine whether they are effective and whether further refinement is required.

These simple steps provide the unifying vision that the wealth holder and selected service providers need. They allow us to bind wisdom and process with principles and standards. They also give us a framework to talk to investment professionals, for the Ethos framework is designed to provide investment professionals the ability to infuse their own work with wisdom and process. Ethos provides a common vocabulary for the different perspectives involved with the wealth management process.

Part 1 of this book has been written for the wealth holder to help him or her consider what wealth management is all about. It frames the central question—*What is the wealth for?*— then provides reflections and philosophy about wealth management.

Part 2 is in effect the user's manual for service providers serving the wealth holder, specifically in the role of the Standards Director. Professionals need to appreciate the Principles set out in Part 1 so that they can speak wisely to the wealth holders; but professionals ultimately need to understand and use the Standards defined in Part 2. The wealth holder will be best served if he or she appreciates the roles and responsibilities of the Standards Director but need not be able to assume those roles and responsibilities.

Principles of Wealth Management for Private Wealth Holders and Related Parties

14

The Standards Director

In Part i we introduced the concept of Global Wealth Management Principles. In this, Part 2, we discuss the Global Wealth Management Standards that have evolved from the Principles. If Part 1 represents the theory, Part 2 represents the practice—Part 2 is intended to be the user's manual.

The central player in Part 2 will be the professional serving in the role of the Standards Director—the professional designated by the wealth holder to ensure that the wealth holder's Principles are fulfilled. In turn, it will be the Standards Director who will manage the other service providers and staff who will be required to implement the wealth management program. The Standards Director will be responsible for developing, implementing, and maintaining the wealth holder's Private Wealth Policy Statement (PWPS; see Appendix)—the business plan for implementing and monitoring the wealth holder's Principles and corresponding Standards.

Because the role of the Standards Director is based on defined standards, the Director's work can be objectively monitored, even audited, to give the wealth holder comfort that the Director is compliant and comfort to live life without engaging in the details of the wealth management program.

The Leadership Role of the Standards Director

The Standards Director may serve in the capacity of an agent, steward, or fiduciary to the wealth holder and is expected to prudently delegate responsibilities to other service providers whenever the Standards Director lacks the time, expertise, or capacity. The Standards Director can be a family employee, a lawyer or an accountant, or anyone trusted by the family.

The actions of the Standards Director as the leader and manager of the wealth management process will have the greatest impact on whether the wealth holder's Principles are accomplished. As the principal agent of change, the Standards Director must have the skills to organize, coordinate, direct, and administer the Standards.

The roles of the Standards Director include the following:

- Encouraging the wealth holder's consideration of what the wealth is for by designing processes that keep that question always visible
- Monitoring and protecting the independence of each family member as appropriate so that through clearly delineated processes wealth holders can self-actualize while at the same time participating as needed to discharge their responsibilities
- Working with and for the wealth holder designing and monitoring strategies (including governance structures, succession plans, education programs, and other strategies) to accomplish stated purposes and to be implemented in a timely manner
- Designing processes to ensure that the wealth holder and any trusts or other entities are fully compliant with best fiduciary practices
- Designing and monitoring compensation plans for staff and outside advisors to ensure transparency and alignment of interests and establishing and monitoring policies relating to prohibition of self-dealing and expectations of loyalty
- Ensuring that service providers are aware of the Principles adopted by the wealth holder and that there are no gaps between the desires of the wealth holder and the intentions and activities of service providers (that is, there is professional integrity across the scope of services)

- Defining job descriptions for the various service providers in terms of *purpose* rather than *function* (For example, a money manager's purpose is to ensure that the wealth holder's portfolio reflects the risk tolerances, asset class preferences, and liquidity requirements of the wealth holder; the money manager's function is to manage a portfolio of stocks and/or bonds.)
- Ensuring that the wealth management team has the appropriate assets and resources (physical, financial, and human) to support the wealth holder's goals and objectives and allocating the assets and resources in an optimum combination
- Preparing and maintaining the wealth holder's Private Wealth Policy Statement and documenting decisions affecting the PWPS as they are made
- Ensuring that due diligence procedures are developed and followed for every service provider
- Making or arranging for periodic assessments of service providers and holding persons accountable, defining rewards and consequences, and insulating the wealth holder from conflicts of interests

Leadership is not a term we ordinarily would associate with a wealth management process; yet, any worthwhile endeavor will always have a leadership component if it is intended to be successful, and wealth management is no exception.

One can rise to a position of leadership by the role or position he or she assumes or by influencing the decisions of others. Leadership, as defined within the context of the role of the Standards Director, is about projecting ethical and objective advice and persuading all parties involved with the wealth management process to follow and to do what is right.

If one were to examine the five most prominent leadership theories found in business literature today, it would become clear that no one theory adequately defines the unique leadership role associated with the Standards Director. However, we could easily describe the ideal Standards Director as being a meld of the five leading theories:

- **Servant leadership:** The Standards Director must understand the needs of the wealth holder and be committed to fulfilling the wealth holder's Principles.

- **Situational leadership:** The Standards Director needs to know how involved the wealth holder wants to be in the wealth management process.
- **Transactional leadership:** The Standards Director must know what rules and regulations will impact the wealth management program.
- **Transformational leadership:** The Standards Director must be willing to stay informed about the best practices of other Standards Directors.
- **Emotional intelligence:** The Standards Director must monitor the feelings and emotions of the wealth holder and use this information to guide the Director's thinking and actions.

To be successful, the Standards Director must:

- Have a sincere commitment and the courage to develop a consensus formulation of the wealth holder's goals and objectives
- Have the discipline to develop long-term strategies and the patience and courage to evaluate events calmly against the backdrop of uncertainty
- Maintain a macro or holistic view and avoid the lure of hot trends and products
- Have a keen eye for identifying and prioritizing strategic issues—focus first on determining the right things to do, and then prioritize what needs to be accomplished
- Have a systematic approach for crafting and choosing between alternative solutions
- Have an understanding of personal and organizational strengths and weaknesses to determine when delegation and outsourcing is appropriate, and provide clear direction to staff, money managers, and service providers

Once the Standards Director has been identified, the next critical step is to define a process to guide his or her activities. The remaining chapters provide this suggested decision-making framework, plus the leadership behaviors that are essential to the Standard Director's unique role. The linking of a decision-making process to defined leadership behaviors is what we refer to as "ethos."

The Ethos Decision-Making Framework

Superior wealth management is the result of developing a prudent decision-making process or strategy and then adhering to it. Only by following a structured decision-making process can one be certain that all critical components of a wealth management strategy are being properly implemented and monitored.

The wealth management decision-making process that is the subject of Part 2 is based on an Ethos framework. Ethos, simply defined, is the link between leadership behaviors, core values, and a decision-making process.

The words *ethos* and *ethics* are derived from the same Greek root word, and there is even a similarity in their definitions. But the words are not always interchangeable, and we can see instances in which they are not even aligned. Both ethos and ethics are based on moral behavior or, in the case of a profession, a set of guiding principles, but that is where the similarities often end.

Ethos is often used in a much broader context and includes the judgment and discernment process of an individual or organization. The fact that a service provider can demonstrate conformity to a code of ethics, even to the Principles defined in this book, does not mean the service provider has a defined ethos and is capable of managing a sound decision-making process or has the capacity to effectively work with other decision makers, particularly the wealth holder. Likewise, the differences between a "bad" and a "good" Standards Director, even the differences between "good" and "great," can be explained in terms of a defined ethos: there is a consistency in the leadership behaviors, core values, and decision-making processes of great Standards Directors.

Ethos provides a decision-making framework that integrates the Principles with the Standards. The Ethos decision-making process incorporates modern investment theory as well as management techniques being employed by some of the largest and most sophisticated investors in the world. The process provides clear guidance to practical, readily identifiable, and easily adaptable procedures.

The Ethos framework offers several advantages. Adhering to this framework enables the wealth holder and appointed Standards Director to accomplish the following goals:

- Transition through the wealth management process at the wealth holder's pace, from a simple understanding of Principles to the more complex Standards
- Bring each Principle and Standard into separate focus so that the wealth holder understands and appreciates the roles and responsibilities of all the parties involved with various components of the wealth management process
- Understand how a new strategy, service, or product fits, or does not fit, within the overall framework
- Analyze each critical element of the strategy, service, or product in isolation, which facilitates the discovery of shortfalls and omissions to a sound wealth management process

The Ethos decision-making framework starts with a simple five-step process (Figure 15.1):

FIGURE 15.1 Ethos Decision-Making Framework

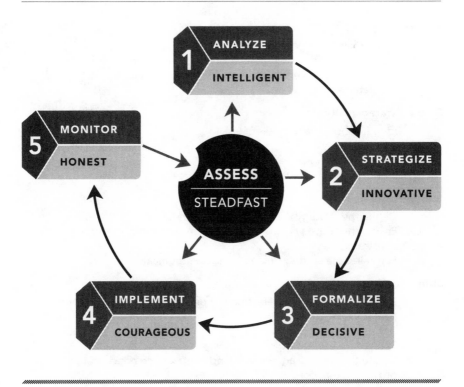

Central to this process is the need to assess performance, effects, and results on an ongoing basis and to make necessary adjustments.

Each of the five steps is then further defined (or refined) by 17 Decision-Making Dimensions. A dimension informs a Standards Director of the level of detail that should be incorporated in the Director's decision-making process (Table 15.1 and Figure 15.2).

TABLE 15.1 Decision-Making Dimensions

Step 1: Analyze

    1.1:   State goals

    1.2:   Define roles and responsibilities of decision makers

    1.3:   Brief decision makers on objectives, standards, policies, and regulations

Step 2: Strategize (RATE)

    2.1:   Identify sources and levels of Risk

    2.2:   Identify Assets

    2.3:   Identify Time horizons

    2.4:   Identify Expected outcomes (performance)

Step 3: Formalize

    3.1:   Define the strategy that is consistent with RATE

    3.2:   Ensure the strategy is consistent with implementation and monitoring constraints

    3.3:   Formalize the strategy in detail and communicate

Step 4: Implement

    4.1:   Define the process for selecting key personnel to implement the strategy

    4.2:   Define the process for selecting tools, methodologies, and budgets to implement the strategy

    4.3:   Ensure that service agreements and contracts do not contain provisions that conflict with objectives

Step 5: Monitor

    5.1:   Prepare periodic reports that compare performance with objectives

    5.2:   Prepare periodic reports that analyze costs, or return on investments, with performance and objectives

    5.3:   Conduct periodic examinations for conflict of interest, self-dealing, and breaches of code of conduct

    5.4:   Prepare periodic qualitative reviews or performance reviews of decision makers

FIGURE 15.2 Step 1 Details and Framework

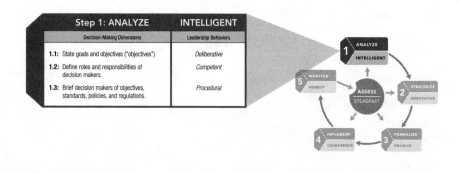

Each of the steps and dimensions has a corresponding leadership behavior—a behavior considered essential for the proper execution of the step or dimension. These are the leadership behaviors we believe are essential for a Standards Director to be effective (Table 15.2 and Figure 15.3).

TABLE 15.2 Essential Leadership Behaviors

Step 1: Analyze

Intelligent
Deliberative
Competent
Procedural

Step 2: Strategize

Innovative
Prudent
Analytical
Patient
Purposeful

Step 3: Formalize

Decisive
Strategic
Pragmatic
Communicative

Step 4: Implement

Courageous
Exemplary
Disciplined
Fair-minded

Step 5: Monitor

Honest
Diligent
Accountable
Genuine
Motivational
Steadfast

FIGURE 15.3 Step 1 Details

Step 1: ANALYZE	INTELLIGENT
Decision-Making Dimensions	Leadership Behaviors
1.1: State goals and objectives ("objectives").	*Deliberative*
1.2: Define roles and responsibilities of decision makers.	*Competent*
1.3: Brief decision makers of objectives, standards, policies, and regulations.	*Procedural*

When the steps, dimensions, and leadership behaviors are woven together, we produce the Ethos framework (Figure 15.4a–c):

FIGURE 15.4A Overview of the Ethos Decision-Making Framework

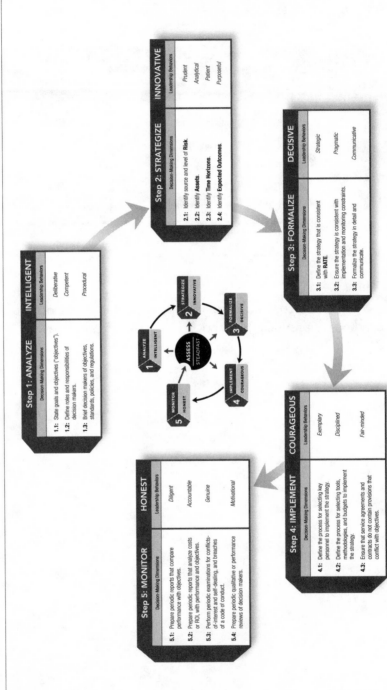

FIGURE 15.4b Central to the Ethos is the Five-Step Decision-Making Process

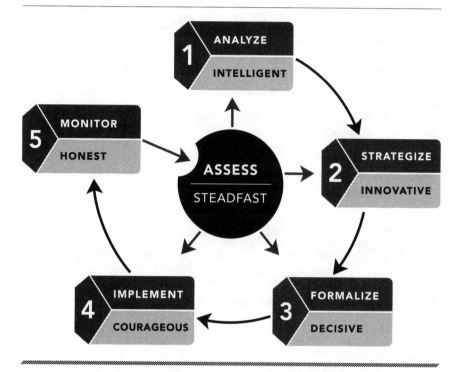

BENEFITS OF A DEFINED ETHOS

Numerous benefits are associated with having a defined Ethos. A defined Ethos:

- Provides the framework for a simple decision-making process, which is a key success factor when operating in a complex and dynamic environment
- Provides the framework to bind Principles, Standards, prudent practices, and procedures, which can be independently assessed and drive performance improvement
- Guides consistent decision making across all levels, which facilitates delegation to staff, money managers, and service providers
- Helps to benchmark current status, prioritize work, and measure progress of the Standards Director
- Helps to uncover procedural and behavioral risks of decision makers

FIGURE 15.4c   Dimensions

Step 1: ANALYZE   INTELLIGENT

Decision-Making Dimensions	Leadership Behaviors
1.1: State goals and objectives ("objectives").	*Deliberative*
1.2: Define roles and responsibilities of decision makers.	*Competent*
1.3: Brief decision makers of objectives, standards, policies, and regulations.	*Procedural*

Step 2: STRATEGIZE   INNOVATIVE

Decision-Making Dimensions	Leadership Behaviors
2.1: Identify source and level of **Risk**.	*Prudent*
2.2: Identify **Assets**.	*Analytical*
2.3: Identify **Time Horizons**.	*Patient*
2.4: Identify **Expected Outcomes**.	*Purposeful*

Step 3: FORMALIZE   DECISIVE

Decision-Making Dimensions	Leadership Behaviors
3.1: Define the strategy that is consistent with **RATE**.	*Strategic*
3.2: Ensure the strategy is consistent with implementation and monitoring constraints.	*Pragmatic*
3.3: Formalize the strategy in detail and communicate.	*Communicative*

Step 4: IMPLEMENT — COURAGEOUS

Decision-Making Dimensions	Leadership Behaviors
4.1: Define the process for selecting key personnel to implement the strategy.	*Exemplary*
4.2: Define the process for selecting tools, methodologies, and budgets to implement the strategy.	*Disciplined*
4.3: Ensure that service agreements and contracts do not contain provisions that conflict with objectives.	*Fair-minded*

Step 5: MONITOR — HONEST

Decision-Making Dimensions	Leadership Behaviors
5.1: Prepare periodic reports that compare performance with objectives.	*Diligent*
5.2: Prepare periodic reports that analyze costs or ROI, with performance and objectives.	*Accountable*
5.3: Perform periodic examinations for conflicts-of-interest and self-dealing, and breaches of a code of conduct.	*Genuine*
5.4: Prepare periodic qualitative or performance reviews of decision makers.	*Motivational*

Added to the Ethos framework are the Standards, which bring the subject of wealth management to life; it is the Ethos framework that helps make the Standards binding to the principles. Together, the elements of the Ethos decision-making framework define a standard of excellence for private wealth management (Figure 15.5).

FIGURE 15.5   Breakdown of the Framework

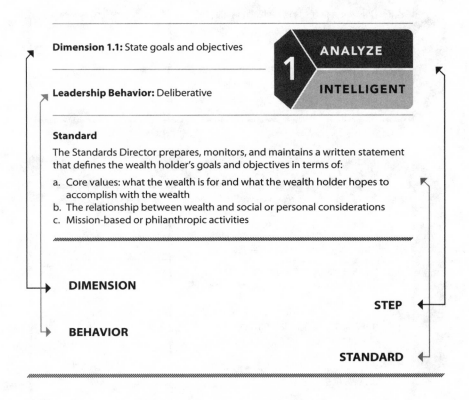

16

Step 1: Analyze

Wisdom and process are the foundations of sound wealth management. The strategies that are implemented must allow the harmonization of all elements of the wealth management operation—from investments to philanthropy to governance to education and well beyond.

Wisdom starts with the understanding of what the wealth is for; until that understanding is developed, there can be no strategy that works. The purpose of the wealth must be articulated individual by individual and may change from time to time. Deciding what the wealth is for and ensuring that it is current is the responsibility of the wealth holder and cannot be delegated. The wealth holder can look to a trusted advisor for help, but ultimately he or she bears the burden of setting out the vision.

Building strategies and following processes, executing the vision of what wealth is for, requires expertise that many wealth holders do not have as well as considerable time and attention that many wealth holders do not want to devote. The management of significant family wealth, like other responsible entities of all kinds, requires proper process to avoid disasters like Madoff, Stanford, and others.

—Chapter 12

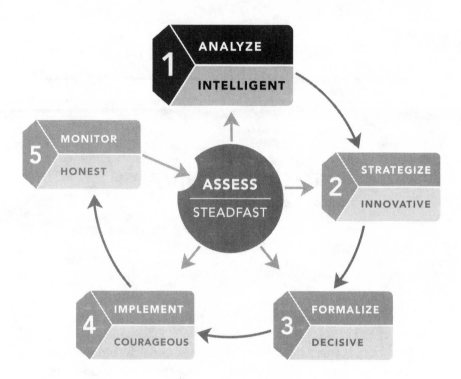

When it comes to the management of significant wealth, the starting question is always, what is the wealth for?

The answer requires a thorough understanding of the wealth holder's current situation, including a complete understanding of the wealth holder's assets and corresponding financial positions; estate planning techniques and structures; current service providers and professional advisors; and philanthropic and legacy interests and objectives. This understanding is obtained from an in-depth analysis of the facts and circumstances pertaining to the wealth holder's goals and objectives.

There are three dimensions to this step (dimensions define the details of a step). Note also the leadership behaviors we believe are essential for the Standards Director to be effective.

Step 1: ANALYZE	INTELLIGENT
Decision-Making Dimensions	Leadership Behaviors
1.1: State goals and objectives ("objectives").	*Deliberative*
1.2: Define roles and responsibilities of decision makers.	*Competent*
1.3: Brief decision makers of objectives, standards, policies, and regulations.	*Procedural*

ESSENTIAL LEADERSHIP BEHAVIOR: INTELLIGENT

Defined as: Great judgment; practical; has the ability to quickly comprehend new information

A Standards Director who has strong "intelligent" skills has a tendency to:

- Absorb, store, and recall new information quickly
- Deal comfortably with abstract concepts and relationships
- Pursue academic, theoretical, or research-based information

A Standards Director who has weak "intelligent" skills has a tendency to:

- Need repetition to process new information
- Prefer concrete tasks
- Learn best through one-on-one instruction

Throughout Part 2, the "strong" and "weak" leadership attributes were developed by The HR Chally Group.

Dimension 1.1: State goals and objectives

Leadership Behavior: Deliberative

ANALYZE

1

INTELLIGENT

Standard

The Standards Director prepares, monitors, and maintains a written statement that defines the wealth holder's goals and objectives in terms of:

a. Core values: what the wealth is for and what the wealth holder hopes to accomplish with the wealth
b. The relationship between wealth and social or personal considerations
c. Mission-based or philanthropic activities.

The goal is the answer to the question, what is the wealth for? Whatever the answer to that question, the journey itself must be planned strategically individual by individual, not as part of some dynastic mandate or under predetermined family criteria. Once the goal is clearly understood, each element of the plan can be managed strategically and guided by wisdom and disciplined process. Every element of the plan of action must be designed, implemented, and monitored to accomplish the goal.

—Chapter 5

As with the running of any formal activity, definitive objectives must be established. Here the Standards Director plays a key management role in ensuring that the wealth holder's goals and objectives are:

♦ Clearly articulated and communicated
♦ Realistic and consistent with current governing documents, estate planning, philanthropic programs, assets, and associated financial positions (liens, loans, and liquidity requirements)

+ A reflection of the wealth holder's view toward wealth and social and personal considerations
+ Aligned with the wealth holder's core values, philanthropic interests, and legacy interests

The Standards Director begins by collecting, reviewing, and analyzing all of the documents and other data pertaining to the management of the wealth holder's affairs:

+ Family-owned businesses
+ Entities of any kind
+ Holdings in real estate and other hard assets
+ Ownership interests in private equity, alternative investments, and hedge funds
+ Existing investment policy statements
+ Philanthropic programs
+ Applicable will, trust, nuptial, and other documents (including amendments)
+ Tax records
+ Custodial and brokerage statements
+ Service agreements with service providers (custodians, money managers, investment consultants, accountants, or attorneys)
+ Information on retained money managers, such as in a prospectus or similar documents
+ Medical records as relevant
+ Any other files pertaining to the management of the wealth holder's assets

The outcome of this initial analysis by the Standards Director should be the establishment of the wealth holder's strategic long-term goals and objectives. The wealth holder's tactical or short-term performance expectations will be identified in Step 2, Dimension 2.4.

The wealth holder's long-term goals and objectives:

◆ Need to align with the resources, capability, and financial situation of the wealth holder

◆ Must be within the limits and constraints of any applicable governing documents and controlling regulatory framework and tax jurisdictions (Dimension 1.3)

◆ Should be periodically assessed in light of current results and conditions and future trends (Step 5)

ESSENTIAL LEADERSHIP BEHAVIOR: DELIBERATIVE

Defined as: Persuasive; ability to build consensus, identify strategic goals and objectives of the wealth holder, and listen to different and opposing opinions in order to galvanize common goals and objectives

A Standards Director who has strong "deliberative" skills has a tendency to:

◆ Keep a focus on defining the wealth holder's goals and objectives, resisting the temptation to interject a personal agenda
◆ Sponsor cooperation and collaboration
◆ Draw ideas and suggestions from all parties
◆ Have a participative style

A Standards Director who has weak "deliberative" skills has a tendency to:

◆ Seek an efficient means to promote a predetermined course of action
◆ See compromise as a weakness
◆ Prefer to make independent decisions
◆ Not feel a responsibility to inspire team building or otherwise engage staff

Dimension 1.2: Define roles and responsibilities of decision makers

ANALYZE

1

INTELLIGENT

Leadership Behavior: Competent

Standard

The Standards Director:

a. Defines in writing the roles and responsibilities of each decision maker and service provider
b. Confirms that each decision maker and service provider demonstrates an awareness of his or her role and responsibilities

---

> A well-run family office can be the temple for the family wealth, where the high priests gather wisdom and follow process to allow everyone to have the blessings of the wealth. A poorly designed family office can actually keep the wealth from doing what it is supposed to do and can become a dark dungeon enslaving the family and all of its members in dysfunction and without wisdom. Whether to have a family office and how to design it requires careful strategic consideration.
>
> —Chapter 9

Successful wealth management professionals have many different approaches, but virtually all develop clear, unambiguous strategies and apply them consistently. This discipline is the key defining behavior of all great wealth managers.

The Standards Director plays the most critical role in the Ethos decision-making process; it is the Standards Director who is the *manager* of the process. But what role will other professionals play, and are they aware of their responsibilities?

To ensure alignment of all parties involved in the decision-making process, each party's role and responsibilities should be communicated in writing, either by a services agreement or in the Private Wealth Policy Statement (Step 3, Dimension 3.3). Alignment enables the Standards Director to delegate with confidence and allows those empowered to act without hesitation.

ESSENTIAL LEADERSHIP BEHAVIOR: COMPETENT

Defined as: Self-assured; having the requisite skills suitable for a defined purpose; ability to lead staff

A Standards Director who has strong "competent" skills has a tendency to:

- Stay abreast of technical developments and review professional publications to stay current on industry best practices
- Apply resources effectively to help reach the goals and objectives of the wealth holder
- Incorporate professional expertise into projects and new initiatives

A Standards Director who has weak "competent" skills has a tendency to:

- Rely on others to be kept updated on technical developments
- Apply an existing body of business principles and applications without taking steps to expand or update it
- Spend an insufficient amount of time tracking key business information sources

Dimension 1.3: Brief decision makers on objectives, standards, policies, and regulations

1   **ANALYZE**

INTELLIGENT

Leadership Behavior: Procedural

Standard

The Standards Director:

a. Defines in writing fiduciary best practices to be followed by all persons serving in a fiduciary capacity
b. Ensures the wealth holder is tax compliant (complying with appropriate standards)
c. Ensures that succession plans are in place for the wealth holder
d. Ensures that reasonable provision is made for succession for those providing advice or service to the wealth holder
e. Secures from legal counsel the appropriateness of wills, charters, trust instruments, appointments of successors, and similar instruments effectuating succession for the wealth holder
f. Establishes or confirms there is a process in place periodically to review the succession plan for the wealth holder and to review succession plans that are in place for others

In fact the ideal family office has many of the following features:

- It is professionally run, possibly building in the efficiencies available when a number of families share professional management and ownership.
- It has a clear plan for succession of management, insulating the family as much as possible from the challenges of replacing departing staff.
- It allows the family to set policy and detail by articulating what it wants of its wealth without requiring the family to manage policy, detail, or implementation.
- It recognizes that the individual is paramount and that the needs of each individual must be met in a customized fashion.

- It can be neutral in judgment with respect to individual needs so that it can serve the needs of many generations, many jurisdictions, and many cultures.
- It accesses "industrial-strength" due diligence but understands and meets individual investment needs.
- It is unconflicted in every respect, and its employees are incentivized by success in helping the wealth achieve its purposes.

—Chapter 9

There are several facets to this dimension: The Standards Director has the responsibility not only to ensure that all decision makers are aware of policies, standards, and regulations that may affect the wealth management strategy but also to ensure that the wealth holder is fulfilling appropriate roles and responsibilities when serving as a personal trustee, as a fiduciary on an investment committee, or as a director on a for-profit or not-for-profit board.

Full discourses on all the regulations or trust laws that may impact a wealth management strategy are beyond the scope of this book. However, the Ethos decision-making process is intentionally designed to define a procedurally prudent process, which often is the requisite standard of care for trustees, fiduciaries, and boards of directors. Ethos is designed to be a global standard of care that can be used to define any of the following:

- Trustee standard
- Fiduciary standard
- Stewardship standard (when a trustee or fiduciary standard is not legally imposed)
- Governance standard (for a board of directors)
- Project management standard (for staff)

Having one effective decision-making framework that can serve multiple purposes reduces the potential for mistakes. When strategies fail, it often is a result of omission rather than commission. It's not what a decision maker did but rather what a decision maker forgot or failed to do.

ESSENTIAL LEADERSHIP BEHAVIOR: PROCEDURAL

Defined as: Supports and has an understanding of standards, procedures, policies, rules, and regulations

A Standards Director who has strong "procedural" skills has a tendency to:

- Remain attentive to changes in industry, legislation, and regulations
- Apply policies and procedures to define a strategy that is consistent with the wealth holder's goals and objectives
- Maintain business and professional proficiency

A Standards Director who has weak "procedural" skills has a tendency to:

- Focus on superfluous aspects of the business
- Rely on others for a superficial understanding of the business
- Stay too focused on a primary area of expertise and not acquire knowledge in critical, but unrelated, disciplines

17

Step 2: Strategize

Comfort cannot come from one plan or one scheme or one decision. Comfort comes with holistic vision, making sure that every element works with every other element, that the entire web of wealth management is integrated, strategic, and accomplishing its goals. Comfort comes when we know that every detail is designed to work in harmony with every other detail in carefully considered processes to take us from what the wealth is for to what we should be doing. Wisdom helps design the processes, wisdom helps us keep our eyes on the goal, and wisdom helps us understand when a specific plan should not give us comfort. Here then is the view we need from the bluffs overlooking the forest to the river beyond.

—Chapter 4

In Step 1, we gathered and analyzed information that was pertinent to the wealth holder's goals and objectives. We identified all of the professionals involved in the management of the wealth strategy, and we reviewed the roles and responsibilities of these decision makers against the backdrop of the Principles developed and adopted by and for the wealth holder.

In this next step, we are going to identify the inputs that will be used to develop the wealth management strategy. There are four

dimensions to this step, and to make it easier to remember the dimensions, we have come up with the acronym RATE:

R Risks; sources and levels
A Assets, asset class preferences, activities and attributes of capital
T Time horizons associated with the wealth holder's goals and objectives
E Expected outcomes; quantifiable short-term objectives

Step 2: STRATEGIZE — INNOVATIVE

Decision-Making Dimensions	Leadership Behaviors
2.1: Identify source and level of **Risk**.	*Prudent*
2.2: Identify **Assets**.	*Analytical*
2.3: Identify **Time Horizons**.	*Patient*
2.4: Identify **Expected Outcomes**.	*Purposeful*

ESSENTIAL LEADERSHIP BEHAVIOR: INNOVATIVE

Defined as: Advanced views; creative; opportunistic; problem solver

A Standards Director who has strong "innovative" skills has a tendency to:

- Be willing to think outside the box to find a solution
- Display sensitivity and genuine interest in understanding the perspectives of others
- Remain engaged until a problem has been resolved

A Standards Director who has weak "innovative" skills has a tendency to:

- Be biased and make judgmental or inappropriate assumptions without analyzing the situation objectively
- Press toward resolution without identifying the root of the problem
- Oversimplify a problem and its solution

Dimension 2.1: Identify sources and levels of risk

Leadership Behavior: Prudent

Standard

The Standards Director prepares, monitors, and maintains a written statement that defines the wealth holder's sources of risk, and the wealth holder's tolerances to each, in terms of:

a. Financial risks
b. Tax and estate risks
c. Family governance risks
d. Hazard risks
e. Operational risks
f. Social, relationship, or entitlement risks

> Almost any wealth creator has faced substantial volatility and uncertainty during the creation of wealth.
>
> —Chapter 7

The analysis of risk often is an important concern among wealth holders. Risk can never be completely avoided, but it can be managed through the proper implementation of a sound decision-making process.

The term *risk* has different connotations depending on the wealth holder's frame of reference, circumstances, and objectives. Typically, the investment industry defines risk in terms of statistical measures such as standard deviation. However, these statistical measures may fail to adequately communicate the potential negative consequences an investment, governance, succession-planning, or other strategy can have on the ability of the wealth holder to meet stated goals and objectives.

Risks are not only financial. They include any impediment to the accomplishments desired and the purposes to be pursued, any threat to happiness and freedom. Poor health can destroy the best-laid plans. For the wealth creator or wealth preserver, time taken away from family can create gaps in life's fulfillment. Models built on wealth creation can obscure a child's understanding of what the wealth is for. Relationships can be placed at risk.

Risk, then, is generally defined as the probability or likelihood that a particular strategy will not achieve the wealth holder's stated goals and objectives (Dimension 1.1). This is the reason the essential leadership behavior for this dimension is "prudent." Applying such a definition means that cash could be riskier than equities if the investment strategy has not been structured to offset the effects of inflation or if a business strategy is abandoned at precisely the wrong time and for the wrong reason because of unwelcomed volatility.

The Standards Director should develop a "risk checklist" and periodically assess what risk factors may be relevant to the wealth holder's situation.

Risks to individuality and freedom include the following:

- **Liquidity risk**—The inability to raise cash when obligations come due.
- **Asset allocation risk**—When the asset mix associated with an investment strategy has a low probability of meeting the wealth holder's goals and objectives.
- **Boardroom risk**—When the wealth holder is facing an increasingly hostile "board of directors," that is, hostility in the family.
- **Purchasing power risk**—The adoption of an investment strategy that will not keep pace with inflation.
- **Lost opportunity risk**—When the right strategy is developed but not implemented: "Yes, I know I should have a larger allocation in equities, but now is not a good time to buy."

The following risk matrix (Table 17.1) also has been developed to help identify potential risks, both internal and external, that may impact the wealth holder's strategy.

TABLE 17.1 Risk Matrix

	Risks That Emanate from Within the Wealth Holder's Domain	Risks That Emanate from Outside the Wealth Holder's Domain
Financial Risks	Lack of liquidity; poor investment process	A change in interest rates; currency risk; tighter credit; change in tax laws
Hazard Risks	A "bad actor" within the family; a dishonest service provider	Natural disasters; terrorist attacks
Operational Risks	Loss of a Standards Director or other key decision maker; embezzlement by key staff; no succession plan	Determination that trust or tax structures are inappropriate; breached contracts; a change in financial regulations; theft
Governance Risks	Divorce; loss of board control of a family-owned business	Geopolitical instability; a dishonest service provider
Social, Relationship, or Entitlement Risks	Family members or service providers acting in their own self-interests or displaying behavior inconsistent with the wealth holder's ethos	Everyone else is doing it; a change in what is considered culturally or politically acceptable

ESSENTIAL LEADERSHIP BEHAVIOR: PRUDENT

Defined as: Wise or judicious in decision making; circumspect in planning and action; controlled work approach

A Standards Director who has strong "prudent" skills has a tendency to:

- Gather considerable evidence prior to adopting new methods or procedures
- Minimize risk by thinking through anticipated consequences
- Be resistant to moving quickly if quality may be jeopardized

A Standards Director who has weak "prudent" skills has a tendency to:

- Embrace experimental ideas without giving sufficient consideration to possible failure or obstacles
- Act with spontaneity and impulsiveness
- Take action before fully comprehending the situation

Dimension 2.2: Identify assets

STRATEGIZE

2

INNOVATIVE

Leadership Behavior: Analytical

Standard

The Standards Director prepares, monitors, and maintains a written statement that defines the wealth holder's assets in terms of:

a. Liquid assets
b. Illiquid assets
c. Business assets
d. Human capital

To have truly diversified liquidity requires a diversified perspective on currency and a diversified perspective on custody. But defining diversification of liquidity will also require strategic analysis in other areas as well. Those who relied on auction rate securities as their portfolio of liquidity were disappointed. Those who relied on Lehman custody for liquidity outside the United States were also disappointed. Greek bonds have proven not as liquid in euro terms as might the bonds of a country actually printing the currency will appear in terms of that currency. Gold is liquid only as long as it is held in an accessible place, only as long as you can withdraw and use it.

—Chapter 7

The Standards Director's role is to decide which of the wealth holder's assets, optimally allocated, will produce the greatest probability of achieving stated goals and objectives (Dimension 1.1). The process begins by taking an inventory of the wealth holder's assets: liquid (cash reserves and other available funding sources), illiquid, business, and human capital (for founders, often considered the most valuable asset). How these assets are deployed among various competing objectives requires a thorough knowledge of:

+ The assets, their availability and usefulness
+ Other available choices and options
+ The risk-reward ratio of deploying (or not deploying) different assets
+ Redeployment or rebalancing as the situation changes (the environment, market, family governance, etc.)

With regard to the identification of assets classes for a traditional investment portfolio, the process begins with a thoughtful discussion on the relative attractiveness of the broad asset classes, ensuring that all decision makers have a good understanding of the risk-return profile of each. As with risk, an asset class discussion can have different connotations, depending on the wealth holder's frame of reference and preferences. For example, a wealth holder could have misplaced confidence or comfort in a fixed-income strategy simply because it is labeled as a bond portfolio—think about the 2008 world economic crisis, and the global fixed-income portfolios that were virtually wiped out because of investments in U.S. mortgage-backed securities.

Once a decision is made regarding the allocations of equities, fixed income, and cash (the primary determinants to the overall risk-return profile of the portfolio), consideration should be given to diversifying the portfolio further into a broader, global mix. A key question that typically emerges at this stage is, what is the appropriate number of asset classes for the investment strategy? The answer depends on the facts and circumstances, including the following variables:

+ **The Standards Director's expertise:** The Standards Director should stick with what he or she knows best and stay clear of any asset classes or strategies where he or she lacks the time, inclination, and knowledge to properly conduct due diligence.
+ **Level of due diligence available:** The asset classes or investment strategies most likely to create the highest return may have such complexity that the wealth holder cannot perform the due diligence necessary for those asset classes or strategies. The Standards Director must evaluate the level of due diligence available and then limit the portfolio to classes and strategies appropriate for that level of due diligence.
+ **Expertise of the wealth holder:** The investment-savvy wealth holder will likely be more willing to accept a more sophisticated investment approach. The less sophisticated wealth holder might accept initial suggestions but may bolt during periods of market volatility.
+ **Sensitivity to fees:** The Standards Director has a responsibility to control and account for all of the expenses associated with the wealth management strategy (Dimension 5.2). More asset classes will mean higher expenses. Does the addition of more asset classes justify the additional expense?

Once the Standards Director has decided on the number of asset classes that should be included in the development of the investment strategy (Dimension 3.1), the question turns to which asset classes should be chosen?

At the risk of oversimplifying a very complex and highly debatable answer, this is how we would build an asset class table (Table 17.2):

TABLE 17.2   Asset Classes

Number of Asset Classes in Strategy	Asset Classes	Added Asset Classes
3	Domestic equity, fixed income, cash	
4	Domestic equity, fixed income, cash	International equity
5	Domestic equity, international equity, fixed income, cash	Small cap (split domestic equity into large cap and small cap)
6	Large-cap equity, small-cap equity, international equity, fixed income, cash	Broad fixed income and intermediate fixed income (split fixed income to broad fixed income and intermediate fixed income)
7	Large-cap equity, small-cap equity, international equity, broad fixed income, intermediate fixed income, cash	Large-cap value and large-cap growth (split large-cap equity into large-cap value and large-cap growth)
8	Large-cap value, large-cap growth, small-cap equity, international equity, broad fixed income, intermediate fixed income, cash	Emerging markets
9	Large-cap value, large-cap growth, small-cap equity, international equity, emerging markets, broad fixed income, intermediate fixed income, cash	Real estate and/or commodities

ESSENTIAL LEADERSHIP BEHAVIOR: ANALYTICAL

Defined as: Ability to identify the different elements or parts of a defined universe; ability to network; team builder

A Standards Director who has strong "analytical" skills has a tendency to:

- Possess strong deductive reasoning skills and is capable of thinking through problems in a systematic and logical manner
- Effectively weigh the accuracy of different types of information, including inferences, abstractions, or generalizations
- Move easily between people or groups to identify opportunities for potential future business contacts

A Standards Director who has weak "analytical" skills has a tendency to:

- Also be weak in networking, being more at ease interacting with established and familiar acquaintances
- Allow biases to prevent him or her from seeing all sides of an issue
- Make decisions according to clearly defined rules
- Rely on like-minded people for input into decisions

Dimension 2.3: Identify time horizons

Leadership Behavior: Patient

Standard

The Standards Director prepares, monitors, and maintains a written statement that defines the wealth holder's time horizon for the management of wealth (e.g., perpetuity; multigenerational).

A family should design its investment policies, processes, and disciplines strategically to meet the family's goals and objectives. The
challenge again is achieving the perspective necessary to see the
destination before selecting the route to get there. Every element
of investment theory, policy, and analytics should work together to
make the wealth do what it is intended to do by helping the wealth
holder accomplish his or her purposes.

—Chapter 7

Another critical role the Standards Director plays is to help ensure
that the investment portfolio has sufficient liquidity to meet financial obligations when they come due.

At a minimum, we suggest the Director prepare a cash-flow statement that shows anticipated contributions and disbursements for, at
least, five years out. Such a cash-flow analysis is essential in determining the *time horizon* of investment portfolios. The identification of the time horizon for each of the wealth holder's various goals
and objectives often is the key variable in determining the allocation between equity and fixed income—between liquid and illiquid
assets. As a general rule, time horizons of less than five years should
be implemented with cash and fixed income, while time horizons
of greater than five years should be allocated across a broad range of
asset classes. Even if the wealth holder has a high risk tolerance, the
Standards Director should not direct an investment in equities if the
money is required by the wealth holder in the next year.

The identification of time horizons will have the most impact on
the hierarchy of investment decisions managed by the Standards
Director:

THE HIERARCHY OF DECISIONS

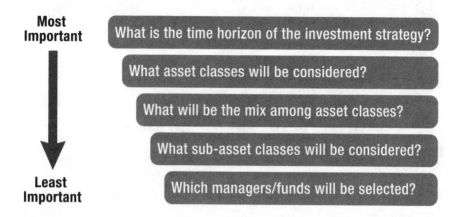

Most Important

What is the time horizon of the investment strategy?

What asset classes will be considered?

What will be the mix among asset classes?

What sub-asset classes will be considered?

Least Important

Which managers/funds will be selected?

There is a hierarchy to the questions the Standards Director has to answer, the most important being what is the time horizon of the wealth holder's various goals and objectives? Based on the time horizons, the Standards Director can then work to determine, in order:

◆ Which asset classes can be appropriately considered
◆ What the allocation should be between the selected asset classes
◆ Whether an allocation should be made among sub-asset classes (i.e., large-cap versus small-cap stocks)
◆ Which money managers or funds should be implemented for each asset class

Note that when unsophisticated wealth holders are left to their own devices, they often reverse the hierarchy of decisions, chasing the latest "hot" manager and, in essence, abdicating their asset allocation decisions to a complete stranger. This is the most common mistake made by the wealth holders who invested with Bernie Madoff.

The Principles set out relating to time horizons and practicality for investment strategy must be applied to every other strategy. For example, in designing educational programs or governance structures, what are time horizons and what must have happened by when? "Even if Rome was not built in a day, the barn door must be closed before the horse escapes," said one patriarch considering whether and how to design a long-term trust to protect his spendthrift progeny.

ESSENTIAL LEADERSHIP BEHAVIOR: PATIENT

Defined as: Ability to prioritize; bears uncertainty (risk) with fortitude and calm; optimistic

A Standards Director who has strong "patient" skills has a tendency to:

- Prioritize and assess situations or tasks with the intent of committing time to the most critical or key objectives regardless of personal preference
- Focus on positive goal attainment and keep obstacles in perspective
- Set realistic goals and deadlines, anticipating barriers

A Standards Director who has weak "patient" skills has a tendency to:

- Set priorities with superficial information or a limited understanding of goals and objectives
- Try to do too much in a given time frame and not anticipate delays
- Feel victimized by setbacks and focus on the problem rather than developing a solution
- Overreact to stress and respond in a nonproductive manner

Dimension 2.4: Identify expected outcomes (performance)

2 STRATEGIZE

INNOVATIVE

Leadership Behavior: Purposeful

Standard

The Standards Director prepares, monitors, and maintains performance objectives in terms of:

a. Long- and short-term performance
b. Absolute returns and outcomes
c. Relative returns and outcomes

When we consider investment performance we often consider return, that is, what percentage increase or decrease has occurred over the relevant time frame. The higher the increase, the greater the return. That is easy to measure mathematically. But any performance to be considered is only partly return; it is also *appropriateness*. For the pension or annuity fund, for the endowment fund, appropriateness takes into account the elements of risk and the requirements of return. For the private wealth holder, appropriateness takes into account whether the investments are appropriate in terms of what the wealth is for.

—Chapter 7

Expected outcomes differ from the wealth holder's goals and objectives identified in Step 1, Dimension 1.1, in that they represent quantifiable results expected to be achieved over a shorter, specified time horizon. For example, an expected outcome may be for an investment strategy to produce a total rate of return that exceeds the rate of inflation by a certain amount or to have sufficient liquidity to pay estate taxes that are coming due.

The identification of expected outcomes serves three purposes:

- They are necessary inputs to the wealth management strategy (Dimension 3.1).
- They are important components to the Private Wealth Policy Statement (Dimension 3.3).
- They facilitate the establishment of benchmarks for the monitoring phase (Dimension 5.1).

The Standards Director is not expected to be able to forecast the future performance of strategies whether with respect to different asset classes or otherwise, but he or she is expected to demonstrate that the strategy is based on thoughtful and realistic performance expectations.

Performance expectations must be articulated for every strategy in terms of "what is reasonable." Creation of a trust does not overnight make an inexperienced trustee a wise trustee no matter how sophisticated the trust instrument. Instead a Standards Director should design (or have designed) a series of steps, chores, or challenges, each to create a realistic experience on which the trustee can build wisdom. A 10-year-old should not be expected to manage cash; a 15-year-old cannot reasonably be expected to perform due diligence on hedging strategies; an artist is not necessarily likely to become an entrepreneur.

In preparing performance expectations, whether they be investment- or business-related, a good general-purpose process to employ is SMART. (The origin or source of SMART is unknown; however, Peter Drucker is credited with first using the acronym in a published paper.) Table 17.3 delineates what the performance expectations should be.

TABLE 17.3   Performance Expectations

S	Specific	Communicates precisely what, when, and how
M	Measurable	Stated in terms of quantity, quality, timeliness, or cost
A	Attainable	Provides an objective that can be aggressively obtained
R	Results-oriented	Relevant and conforming to the wealth holder's goals and objectives
T	Time-bound	Beginning, end, and specific milestones are defined

ESSENTIAL LEADERSHIP BEHAVIOR: PURPOSEFUL

Defined as: Determined, directed toward a specific outcome; portfolio focused

A Standards Director who has strong "purposeful" skills has a tendency to:

- Develop a solid relationship with the wealth holder, making the wealth holder's goals and objectives a priority
- Build a thorough knowledge of the wealth holder
- Recognize that the wealth holder's goals and objectives may change and be willing to adjust business plans to address the changing requirements

A Standards Director who has weak "purposeful" skills has a tendency to:

- Treat the relationship with the wealth holder in a functional manner rather than developing an intimate knowledge of the wealth holder's goals and objectives
- Focus more on the administrative aspects of the job rather than on adapting business strategies to accommodate the wealth holder's needs
- Build relationships with other wealth holders who are easily satisfied

(18)

Step 3: Formalize

Once the wealth holder or family develops the principles, their implementation can be accomplished by standards and a business plan that allows all of those involved to know the rules, clearly and uniquely set out to support the principles. The standards need to be developed by independent and objective professionals who have the capacity and training to set out the management of each principle. Tools and resources can then be allocated to ensure that select service providers can do their jobs efficiently and effectively. Once the business plan is created, it can be monitored, assessed, and modified over time, and professionals running the family wealth can be evaluated objectively by the wealth holder or others.

—Chapter 13

In Step 1, we defined the long-term goals and objectives of the wealth holder. We identified the professionals who would be involved in the wealth management process; and we ensured that decision makers were aware of their roles and responsibilities as well as of the standards, regulations, and policies that would impact the investment process.

In Step 2, we gathered the information that would be critical to the development of the wealth management strategy:

R Risk tolerances
A Asset, asset class preferences, activities and attributes of capital
T Time horizon
E Expected outcomes

In Step 3, we're going to develop the wealth management strategy that:

♦ Represents the greatest probability of achieving the wealth holder's goals and objectives
♦ Is consistent with the wealth holder's unique risk-return profile
♦ Is consistent with the Standards Director's implementation and monitoring constraints

Once these requirements are satisfied, the Standards Director has the inputs to prepare the wealth holder's Private Wealth Policy Statement (PWPS).

Step 3: FORMALIZE	DECISIVE
Decision-Making Dimensions	Leadership Behaviors
3.1: Define the strategy that is consistent with **RATE**.	*Strategic*
3.2: Ensure the strategy is consistent with implementation and monitoring constraints.	*Pragmatic*
3.3: Formalize the strategy in detail and communicate.	*Communicative*

ESSENTIAL LEADERSHIP BEHAVIOR: DECISIVE

Defined as: Resolute; determined; assertive; competitive

A Standards Director who has strong "decisive" skills has a tendency to:

+ Mix both logic and human factors in negotiating disagreement
+ Be capable of disagreeing without intimidation
+ Be consistent and predictable in asserting himself or herself, rather than acting aggressively or passively without warning

A Standards Director who has weak "decisive" skills has a tendency to:

+ Be reluctant to disagree for fear of being seen as disagreeable
+ Avoid emotional argument
+ Allow frustration to build when backing down from repetitive negative issues

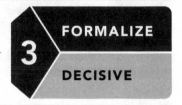

Dimension 3.1: Define the strategy that is consistent with RATE

Leadership Behavior: Strategic

Standard

The Standards Director defines in writing the wealth management strategy that is consistent with:

a. Risk tolerances
b. Asset class preferences (taking into consideration the wealth holder's other assets)
c. Mission-based or philanthropic objectives (if defined in Dimension 1.1)
d. Time horizons
e. Performance objectives
f. Rebalancing guidelines

> Strategic design of a portfolio thus starts long before asset allocation.... That means at a given time, a portfolio of 90 percent equities can make sense for one person while a portfolio of 10 percent equities can make sense for another. Neither percentage comes from a hard-and-fast rule that should apply to every investor. Each reflects a notion of appropriateness designed for the particular investor.
>
> —Chapter 7

Once the Standards Director knows the wealth holder's goals and objectives and has determined the inputs to RATE (Dimensions 2.1–2.4), the Director is ready to define the strategies that produce the greatest probability of achieving the wealth holder's goals and objectives. Considerable research and experience has shown that the choice of assets (staff, service providers, and money managers) and asset classes, and subsequent allocation of each, will have more impact on the long-term performance of the wealth management strategy than any other factor.

How assets are deployed among various competing objectives requires a thorough knowledge of the following topics:

+ The assets, their availability and usefulness
+ Other available choices and options
+ The risk-reward ratio of deploying (or not deploying) different assets
+ Redeployment or rebalancing as the market or the portfolio's situation changes

At this point, it may be worthwhile to comment on the use of optimization (i.e., asset allocation) software when developing an investment strategy. Yes, a Standards Director needs to have access to good asset allocation tools—particularly in determining the allocation between equities, fixed income, and cash. However, due to the great disparity between different software offerings and services provided by investment consultants, we would caution Directors to carefully research the investment expertise of the software developer or the investment consultant. The old adage "garbage in, garbage out" has never been more applicable.

Most asset allocation strategies are driven by three inputs:

+ The modeled or expected risk (standard deviation of returns) of each asset class
+ The modeled or expected return of each asset class
+ The modeled or expected correlations of each asset class's return with that of the other asset classes

The Standards Director's responsibility is to ensure that these expected or modeled inputs are reasonable, which is no easy task. Experience suggests that historical data on different asset classes appears to be quite useful with respect to developing standard deviation estimates, "reasonably useful for correlations, and virtually useless for expected returns" (William Sharpe, Nobel Prize–winning economist). Simple extrapolations of historical data are not only likely to be poor estimates of future performance but also may lead to the development of expectations that cannot be met.

Over the years, we have seen investment decision makers make one or more of the following mistakes when developing an asset allocation strategy:

+ Believing that asset allocation is a science and accepting a level of precision or confidence that simply is unwarranted. There is still an element of art and uncertainty involved in the development of an appropriate asset strategy. Once the critical allocations have been made between equity, fixed income, and cash, the allocation to additional asset classes can be determined with common sense through an intuitive process. Despite advances in portfolio modeling, not all asset allocation decisions have been reduced to a computerized solution.
+ Not informing the wealth holder of how the asset allocation helps accomplish what the wealth is for. If the wealth holder does not fully understand the strategy, it is likely he or she will want to bolt at the first sign of market volatility.
+ Underallocating. Making an allocation of less than 5 percent rarely makes good sense for two reasons: (1) it probably will not materially change the risk-return profile of the wealth holder's portfolio, and (2) it will be costly, in terms of both implementation and monitoring.
+ Making an allocation to an asset that the Standards Director cannot properly implement or monitor (discussed further in Dimension 3.2). The classic example is an allocation to hedge funds. Because of the lack of transparency and the complexity of the financial instruments employed, the Director may not be able to employ the same level of due diligence as could be applied to a traditional money manager. *If the Standards Director lacks the time, inclination, or knowledge to conduct appropriate due diligence—be it of an asset class or an investment manager—he or she should stay clear of the strategy or the manager.*

ESSENTIAL LEADERSHIP BEHAVIOR: STRATEGIC

Defined as: Ability to multitask over a protracted period; accurate; focused; has situational awareness

A Standards Director who has strong "strategic" skills has a tendency to:

- Collect and organize data quickly and intuitively and then analyze and prioritize conflicting goals
- Simultaneously juggle several projects efficiently, despite constraints on time or resources
- Initiate action promptly, despite uncertainty of outcome; make the best decision possible at any given point in time
- Formulate contingency plans to cover any unexpected ramifications

A Standards Director who has weak "strategic" skills has a tendency to:

- Prefer to tackle priorities consecutively, bringing one to completion before starting another
- Defer a decision until all the options are completely evaluated
- Selectively search for data that supports a predetermined opinion or supposition
- Be satisfied with superficial planning rather than pursue alternatives

Dimension 3.2: Ensure the strategy is consistent with implementation and monitoring constraints

Leadership Behavior: Pragmatic

Standard

The Standards Director ensures that the asset allocation and investment strategy are consistent with the Standards Director's implementation and monitoring constraints.

> If wealth is about freedom, convoluted investment strategies are rarely strategic. There can be no process, little delegatable, and no likelihood that the wealth holder will fully understand what he or she is investing in. The complexity alone can deprive family members of feelings of freedom. Instead they spend time trying to understand what they cannot and feeling unsure whether they should trust those running the investments. How can a person pursue passions to self-actualization if he or she is busy in a maze of derivatives and jargon?
>
> —Chapter 7

What starts out as strategy must be translated into reality with implementation, and what is implemented needs to be monitored. The proposed wealth management strategy (Dimension 3.1) now must be carefully evaluated to determine whether the suggested strategy can be prudently implemented (discussed in more detail in Dimension 4.1) and then effectively and efficiently monitored (discussed in more detail in Dimension 5.1) on an ongoing basis.

One demonstrates prudence by the process through which one manages wealth management decisions. No strategy is imprudent on its face. It is the way in which it is used, and the way decisions regarding its use are made, that will be examined to determine whether the prudence test has been met. Even the most aggressive and unconventional strategy can meet the standard if arrived at through a sound process, while the most conservative and traditional one may not measure up if a sound process is lacking.

The greatest risk in the development of any strategy is omission—leaving out something vital. This is why standards and a defined decision-making process, such as the one provided in this book, are so critical.

At this point, the Standards Director should be able to demonstrate that he or she has documented the following inputs that are going to be used to develop the wealth management strategy:

+ The current and projected resources and obligations of the wealth holder
+ The rationale for the choice of performance goals, time horizons, and permissible asset classes and the sensitivity to variations in each
+ The basis for the validity of the capital markets data utilized in determining the asset allocation

In his book on Winston Churchill, *Churchill on Leadership*, Steven Hayward outlines several rules for effective decision making that Churchill followed:

> Always keep the central or most important aspect of the current problem in mind, know how to balance the chances [risk] on both sides of a decision, and keep these factors in proportion; and remain open to changing your mind in the presence of new facts.
>
> Don't try to look too far ahead, try for excessive perfection, or make decisions for decision's sake that would better be postponed or not made at all.
>
> Churchill's philosophy in managing important decisions also applies to wealth management. Every decision comes with a certain amount of risk, and not every decision will yield a perfect outcome. Success is achieved by seeking out the realistic balance between risk and reward.

ESSENTIAL LEADERSHIP BEHAVIOR: PRAGMATIC

Defined as: Realistic; sensible; politically astute; team-oriented

A Standards Director who has strong "pragmatic" skills has a tendency to:

- ◆ Recognize that the wealth holder can view the same objective or priority differently and is careful not to push his or her own agenda
- ◆ Build cooperative and supportive relationships with other decision makers
- ◆ Understand and align actions and strategies with regulations and compliance requirements

A Standards Director who has weak "pragmatic" skills has a tendency to:

- ◆ Underestimate the need to be politically savvy in meshing his or her objectives with those of the wealth holder's
- ◆ Function more as an individualist than as a team player
- ◆ Prefer to exercise personal control over results and outcomes
- ◆ Believe compromise for the sake of cooperation can potentially threaten the quality of a project

---

Dimension 3.3: Formalize the strategy in detail and communicate

Leadership Behavior: Communicative

Standard

The Standards Director ensures that, for each entity and individual, there is defined in writing a Private Wealth Policy Statement (PWPS).

A family should design its investment policies, processes, and disciplines strategically to meet the family's goals and objectives. The challenge again is achieving the perspective necessary to see the destination before selecting the route to get there. Every element of investment theory, policy, and analytics should work together to make the wealth do what it is intended to do by helping the wealth holder accomplish his or her purposes.

—Chapter 7

In our opinion, the preparation and ongoing maintenance of the wealth holder's Private Wealth Policy Statement (PWPS) is the most important function performed by the Standards Director. So critical is this role, we have prepared a sample PWPS template (see Appendix) based on the Ethos framework.

The PWPS should be viewed as the business plan and the essential management tool for directing and communicating the activities of the wealth management strategy. It should be a formal, long-range, strategic plan that allows the Standards Director to coordinate the management of the strategy within a logical and consistent framework. All material facts, assumptions, and opinions should be included. Although we seem to focus on the investment strategy, the Standards Director can use the guidance here relating to investment strategy as a road map to consideration of every strategy to be used. Similar treatment must be implemented as business planning for philanthropic programs, for capitalization guidelines, for governance, for family values and legacy communication, and for education. All of these aspects of the family wealth program must be considered in the PWPS.

The Standards Director needs to develop the PWPS with the understanding that it will be implemented in a complex and dynamic environment. The PWPS will produce the greatest benefits during periods of adverse conditions, acting as a stabilizer for decision makers who otherwise would be tempted to alter the sound strategy because of irrational fears. Its mere existence will cause decision makers to pause and consider the external and internal circumstances that prompted the development of the PWPS in the first place. This is what the substance of good policy development is all about: the framework and process that will allow cooler heads and a longer-term outlook to prevail.

In periods of financial market prosperity, almost any investment program, no matter how ad hoc its strategy, will likely generate impressive results. In those circumstances, the advantages of a comprehensive PWPS and the time devoted to its development may appear to be marginal. However, even under favorable market conditions, the PWPS may reduce the temptation to increase the aggressiveness of an investment program as other decision makers attempt to extrapolate positive current market trends into the future.

There are a number of reasons why the PWPS is so critical:

+ The PWPS provides logical guidance during periods of uncertainty.
+ The PWPS provides a paper trail of polices, practices, and procedures that can serve as critical evidence used in the defenses against accusations of imprudence or mismanagement.
+ The PWPS provides a baseline from which to monitor performance of overall strategies, as well as the performance of the Standards Director.
+ For estate planning purposes, the PWPS should be included and coordinated with other estate planning documents, providing less sophisticated heirs and executors appropriate guidance for continuing the prudent management of the wealth management strategy.

The PWPS should combine elements of planning and philosophy and should address all five steps of the Ethos process. The sample PWPS included in the Appendix has the following main sections and subheadings (note that the PWPS follows the same structure as the Ethos decision-making framework):

Section I: Definitions
Section II: Purpose
Section III: Statement of Principles
Section IV: Duties and Responsibilities
Section V: Ethics Statement
Section VI: Persons Serving in a Fiduciary Capacity

Section VII: Inputs Used to Develop the Wealth Management
    Strategy
Section VIII: Money Manager and Custodian
Section IX: Monitoring Procedures
Section X: Review of the PWPS

Others may be required depending on the wealth holder or the family. Use this framework as a starting point.

ESSENTIAL LEADERSHIP BEHAVIOR: COMMUNICATIVE

Defined as: Articulate and persuasive in the written and spoken word; effective in both formal and informal communication; cordial and having a sense of humor

A Standards Director who has strong "communicative" skills has a tendency to:

- Customize communication to the understanding of the wealth holder
- Be sensitive to feedback from the wealth holder and adjust communications to sustain the wealth holder's interest
- Take the time to prepare a presentation, injecting content with which the wealth holder can associate and identify
- Recognize the need for thoroughness and accuracy in communicating or documenting information in a written format

A Standards Director who has weak "communicative" skills has a tendency to:

- Fail to incorporate key wealth holder inputs into presentations or respond effectively to the wealth holder's reactions
- Attempt a one-size-fits-all communication style that does not account for different wealth holders' needs
- Keep the wealth holder at arm's length, making presentations seem less personal
- Fail to effectively organize written communications

19

Step 4: Implement

Any investment program requires due diligence to ensure that policies can be implemented with discipline. Performing due diligence is always daunting. The volatility, chicanery, and uncertainty of 2008 and 2009 have made that task seem almost impossible. Indeed, one might say that today due diligence is the gold standard of investment management. It has become the most important function to execute well to ensure the proper management of significant wealth. Due diligence is broader than simply investigating and monitoring investment managers. Due diligence in its broadest terms is ensuring that all assumptions are correct, that all assets believed to be owned are owned, that all risks are considered, and that all facts are as they are represented. The question to ask yourself is, "Have I considered every risk and do I have the information I need to evaluate every risk?"

—Chapter 7

In the previous step, we discussed how to develop a wealth management strategy based on the wealth holder's RATE inputs; ensure that the strategy was consistent with the Standards Director's implementation and monitoring constraints; and prepare the business plan for managing the strategy—the PWPS.

What starts out as strategy must be translated into reality with implementation. Step 4 includes an overview of a due diligence

177

process that can be used to select money managers and service providers, whether lawyers, accountants, advisors, employees, or others; procedures on how to select the right investment vehicle (separate account manager, mutual fund, or commingled trust) to implement the investment strategy; procedures to ensure that service agreements and contracts with employees and service providers do not have provisions that conflict with the wealth management strategy; procedures to align loyalty and prevent self-dealing; procedures to govern philanthropic grants and programs; and procedures relating to how to consider governance, capitalization standards, values and legacy, and next generation education.

Step 4: IMPLEMENT   COURAGEOUS

Decision-Making Dimensions	Leadership Behaviors
4.1: Define the process for selecting key personnel to implement the strategy.	*Exemplary*
4.2: Define the process for selecting tools, methodologies, and budgets to implement the strategy.	*Disciplined*
4.3: Ensure that service agreements and contracts do not contain provisions that conflict with objectives.	*Fair-minded*

ESSENTIAL LEADERSHIP BEHAVIOR: COURAGEOUS

Defined as: Willingness to face risk and uncertainty; deals effectively with stress

A Standards Director who has strong "courageous" skills has a tendency to:

- Remain calm and focused on the wealth holder's goals and objectives
- Be resilient and not take problems as personal affronts
- Keep a sense of perspective in the face of adversity

A Standards Director who has weak "courageous" skills has a tendency to:

- Feel a lack of control and predictability about potential barriers to desired outcomes
- Get flustered easily by the unexpected
- Overreact to stress and respond in a nonproductive manner

Dimension 4.1: Define the process for selecting key personnel to implement the strategy

IMPLEMENT

4

COURAGEOUS

Leadership Behavior: Exemplary

Standard

The Standards Director defines a process for selecting money managers, which includes, at a minimum, the following due diligence screens:

a. The money manager has a defined investment strategy that is consistent with the goals and objectives of the wealth holder and can be understood and monitored by others.
b. The money manager provides transparency of investment holdings.
c. The same investment management team has been in place for a period commensurate with the period of the performance evaluation.
d. Securities in the portfolio are consistent with the stated investment strategy and are liquid.
e. Investment performance has been verified by an independent third party and compared to the money manager's peers.
f. Investment performance adjusted for risk has been compared to the money manager's peers.
g. The money manager's fees and expenses have been compared to the money manager's peers.
h. The investment structure (separate account, mutual fund, commingled trust, or hedge fund) is appropriate for the given strategy and the Standards Director's ability to monitor the strategy.

The Standards Director also defines a process for evaluating custodians and broker-dealers, which includes, at a minimum, the following:

a. As a best practice, custodians are independent of money managers, except as may be required by trust law, or by the necessity of employing a commingled investment vehicle.
b. Custodian can provide appropriate security of assets, with insurance or otherwise.
c. Custodial statements provide sufficient detail that the Standards Director can monitor the money manager's best execution of trades (generation of soft dollars).
d. The expense ratio of the custodian's cash sweep and money market fund is compared to peers.
e. Custodian can provide investment performance reports and tax reporting.

Whether and how a private wealth holder diversifies managers must be considered strategically. It is not easy to diversify managers without a sound due diligence process to analyze the managers individually and in relationship to each other. One must consider the following questions:

◆ Does the manager's philosophy seem sound and do you understand it?

◆ Is the manager's operation and history consistent with that philosophy or style?

◆ Does the manager do what it says it does?

◆ Are the manager's benchmarks reasonable?

◆ Will the manager understand the wealth holder well enough to customize his or her portfolio to meet that individual's needs?

◆ How do the manager's portfolios relate to one another?

—Chapter 7

This dimension continues with the decision-making process involved in implementing the wealth management strategy, specifically the development of due diligence criteria for selecting money managers.

Effective management skills are most critical at this stage, not because the Standards Director needs to become the money manager—just the opposite. We would strongly encourage Directors to follow the time-proven maxim of doing what one does best and delegating the rest to other qualified professionals. The Director's primary function is to set the overall strategy, and the primary function of the money manager is to maximize returns within the parameters defined by that strategy.

The ability to develop uniform search criteria that can be applied to each and every asset class is difficult, and it is made even more challenging if you are considering managers from different countries subject to different rules and regulations. Nevertheless, it is strongly suggested that the Standards Director develop a process that (1) can be consistently applied in any manager search; (2) can be easily communicated to the wealth holder; and (3) can be used in both the search and monitoring phases of the decision-making process.

The Standards Director should keep in mind several points when developing due diligence criteria:

+ Simple is preferable to complex when operating in a complex and dynamic environment (same philosophy used to develop the decision-making framework described in this book).
+ Know the strengths and weaknesses of the various databases. For example, if separate account manager returns are being reported by a database provider, have the returns been independently verified, or were they provided by the manager?
+ Know how peer groups have been constructed, particularly when comparing information on two managers who are providing performance comparisons from two different database providers. Was the manager's peer group based on the manager's returns being correlated with other managers, or were they based on the actual holdings of the manager?
+ When comparing managers, make sure statistics are compared with the same end points (time periods) and benchmarks (e.g., both compared to the S&P 500, instead of one to the S&P 500 and the other to the Russell 1000).

Suggested Due Diligence Process

The following (Tables 19.1–19.4) is a comprehensive due diligence process. It is intended to provide the Standards Director both the breadth and depth of an institutional approach. The Director probably will need to consult more than one database to conduct this thorough due diligence process, so the best advice is to start with a handful of the criteria (for example, risk-adjusted performance and consistency to peer group) to come up with a short list (six to ten candidates), and then apply the more comprehensive process to identify the finalists.

TABLE 19.1   Due Diligence Process: Organization

Professionals	Same portfolio team in place for a period commensurate with performance evaluation period. Rationale: It makes little sense to analyze performance returns for a portfolio management team that is no longer in place or has materially changed in composition.
Depth	There are two parts: (1) the capacity to handle the type of investment strategy proposed (such as a tax-sensitive strategy); and (2) the capacity to handle growth in assets under management. Rationale: (1) Certain investment strategies need more personal money manager oversight. Here the Standards Director's role is to serve as matchmaker and ensure that money managers are willing to work with the proposed wealth management strategy. (2) Some managers may not be able to absorb the growth—in terms of both portfolio servicing and investment strategy. For example, small-cap managers may begin to struggle when they get to $1 billion under management.
Fee Structure	Fees and expenses compare favorably to those of peers, and the manager has a stated policy for managing "soft dollars" and directed brokerage mandates. Rationale: Fees do matter—in our opinion they matter a lot—and a high fee schedule that is accompanied by marginal performance should be unacceptable. As for soft dollars and directed brokerage, both are subject to abuse, so make sure that the manager has a clearly stated policy that indicates both are closely monitored.
Reputation	The firm has no outstanding legal judgments or past judgments that may reflect negatively on the firm. Rationale: The investment industry is based on trust; once lost it can take years for a firm to regain its reputation. During the recovery phase, the firm may find it difficult to retain and recruit top people.

TABLE 19.2 Due Diligence Process: Philosophy/Strategy

Behaviors	The manager must be able to demonstrate that the same strategy or style has been consistently applied and that portfolio holdings are consistent with the stated strategy or style.
	Rationale: The money manager should be hired to fulfill a specific role within the overall investment strategy and should fill a slot defined by a specific risk-reward profile. If the manager floats between styles, it will be difficult to know whether the overall wealth management strategy is aligned to meet the wealth holder's goals and objectives. Furthermore, the performance evaluation and monitoring will be complicated by the fact that the manager may be compared to inappropriate peers and indices.
Buy Discipline	The manager must be able to clearly articulate the buy discipline that will be followed and demonstrate that the strategy has been successfully adhered to over time.
	Rationale: The Standards Director is the manager of the overall process; it is the Director's responsibility to be intimately familiar with each investment process. If the Director doesn't understand the manager's strategy, the Director should move on to a money manager who can provide greater comfort.
Sell Discipline	The manager must be able to clearly articulate the sell discipline that will be followed and demonstrate that the strategy has been successfully adhered to over time.
	Rationale: From our experience, managers have an easier time buying. The more difficult task is knowing when to sell.
Use of Cash	The manager must be able to demonstrate that the manager is not a market timer.
	Rationale: Managers who routinely hold more than 20 percent in cash need to demonstrate that the cash is being held in reserve for buying opportunities, as opposed to being used for market timing.
Turnover	Portfolio turnover is compared to those of peers, is appropriate for taxable portfolios, and does not generate excessive transaction costs.
	Rationale: Turnover is largely an issue for taxable portfolios, but even for tax-exempt portfolios an unusually high turnover will drive up the costs of managing the portfolio. Also, a high turnover should be analyzed to determine whether it is consistent with the manager's stated strategy, because a high turnover also could be an indication of turmoil on the portfolio management team.

TABLE 19.3 Due Diligence Process: Return Performance

Consistency	Returns are evaluated on a quarterly, one-, three-, and five-year basis and are favorable in both rising and falling markets. Rationale: Isolating reviews to three- and five-year performance may obscure short-term volatility. On the other hand, short-term performance is rarely a reliable indicator of strong long-term performance. Both long-term and short-term performance needs to be analyzed for consistency. From experience, the manager who is consistently just above average typically will end up producing stronger long-term performance than peers who are at the top of the charts two years in row and drop to the bottom of the charts the third year.
Relative	Returns are evaluated on a quarterly, one-, three-, and five-year basis and are favorable in comparison to an appropriate index and peer group. Rationale: The trick is ensuring that the manager is measured against the right index and peer group. Here, the focus is on dispersion—unusually high and low returns compared to peers may be a good indication that the manager is in the wrong peer group.
Results	Performance has been calculated by an objective third party. Rationale: (1) The third party should be able to provide a more robust background universe for comparing the manager to peers; and (2) an independent audit is almost always preferable to a self-audit. The same holds true for performance evaluations.

TABLE 19.4   Due Diligence Process: Risk Performance

Control	The manager must be able to clearly articulate the risk strategy that will be followed and demonstrate that the strategy has been successfully adhered to over time. Rationale: Whether the Standards Director is asking the manager about buy or sell disciplines or the manager's risk strategy, the manager should be able to articulate a process that the Director can understand and be able to demonstrate that the strategy has been consistently applied.
Risk-Adjusted Returns	Risk-adjusted returns, whether measured by Alpha, Sharpe, or Sortino ratios, are favorable to those of peers. Rationale: Though appearing low on the due diligence list, it is perhaps one of the more critical components. Performance adjusted for the risk the manager took, and then compared to peers, speaks volumes about the manager's ability.
Results	Risk-adjusted performance has been calculated by an objective third party. Rationale: As with the performance numbers, a best practice is to analyze risk-adjusted performance figures that have been prepared by an independent third party.

Another service provider that needs to be prudently selected is the custodian for the investment portfolio—a greatly unappreciated key player—for the choice of custodian will greatly impact the quality of the monitoring of the wealth management strategy (Step 5).

In considering custodians, a wealth holder must apply due diligence to determine the distinctions among custodians based on business organization, business model, and jurisdiction of incorporation. The old belief that banks are safer than brokers may be misplaced in a world where banks are brokers and brokers are banks; structural and auditing differences can exist between two companies in the same business so that in fact Schwab may be quite different from Fidelity with respect to security of assets held. Even after the due diligence is finished, the conclusions will not be clear. Then it becomes reasonable to have several custodians to protect against failure of one.

—Chapter 7

The role of the custodian is to:

+ Maintain separate accounts by legal registration
+ Value the holdings
+ Collect all income and dividends
+ Settle all transactions (buy-sell orders) initiated by money managers
+ Provide monthly reports that detail transactions, cash flows, securities held and their current value, and change in value of each security and the overall portfolio since the previous report

In conducting due diligence on the custodian, consider the following:

+ What is the quality of the custodian's electronic protocol (connection between the Standards Director, money managers, and the custodian), such as ease of use and the frequency of their updates?
+ What is the expense ratio of the money market accounts attached to the portfolio's account? (If one doesn't ask, the cash portion of a portfolio most likely will be invested in a retail money market account; ask and often the cash can be invested in an institutional share class that will have a considerably lower expense ratio.)
+ Will the custodian provide tax reporting and performance measurement services? (As with the money market accounts, often one has to inquire and, if negotiated at the start of the engagement, may be provided at no extra charge.)
+ Will the custodian provide a monthly statement that provides the details of any trading that was conducted by the money managers? [The details are necessary for the Standards Director to properly monitor whether the manager is seeking best price and execution in trading the portfolio's account (Dimension 5.2).]

ESSENTIAL LEADERSHIP BEHAVIOR: EXEMPLARY

Defined as: Self-starter; shows initiative; loyal and supportive; has the ability and bearing that sets the standard of excellence

A Standards Director who has strong "exemplary" skills has a tendency to:

- Focus effort and resources on initiatives or solutions that will positively contribute to the goals and objectives of the wealth holder
- Champion new initiatives and identify opportunities or issues requiring change without prompting
- Introduce and implement solutions through spheres of influence

A Standards Director who has weak "exemplary" skills has a tendency to:

- Leave "good enough" alone and conform to established rules and principles
- Wait for negative situations to settle over time or to correct themselves
- Be conservative and traditional and not champion new projects
- Be uncomfortable initiating change or trying new approaches without directives from a higher authority

---

Dimension 4.2: Define the process for selecting tools, methodologies, and budgets to implement the strategy

Leadership Behavior: Disciplined

Standard

The Standards Director defines a process to periodically evaluate the process for selecting tools, methodologies, and budgets to implement strategies.

Effective diversification of managers requires hard work, transparency, and complete understanding of manager after manager. Substantial due diligence infrastructure must be in place if one is to gain strategic benefit from diversifying managers. Is the wealth holder willing to invest the time and effort to build or secure that infrastructure? Does the wealth holder have the capacity to insist on full transparency? If the infrastructure is to be outsourced, is the wealth holder willing to invest the time and effort in evaluating managers of managers or consultants, and are the "industrial-strength" consultants actually available?

—Chapter 7

Now that the Standards Director has defined the wealth management strategy (Dimension 3.1) and identified the money managers to implement the strategy (Dimension 4.1), the next two decisions that need to be prudently managed are:

- Whether to implement an asset class with a passive or active strategy
- Whether to engage a manager on a separate account basis or through a mutual fund or commingled trust

Active Versus Passive Investment Strategies

Much has been written about the virtues of passive investing, and we cannot add to the arguments that have been made by more scholarly authorities. However, here are what we believe to be the salient arguments:

- It's not an "either/or" decision. Prudent investors will use both passive and active strategies in a portfolio.
- If the wealth holder is indifferent regarding the use of active or passive strategies, go passive in implementing the large-cap, core portions of the investment strategy. Use active managers in small-cap mandates or emerging markets, where managers have a greater probability of finding a gold nugget that has not been discovered by all the research analysts who are focused on the large-cap stocks.

Separate Account Managers Versus
Mutual Funds or Commingled Trusts

The portfolio's account size may limit the wealth holder's choices to a mutual fund or commingled trust. But improved electronic protocol among managers, custodians, and intermediaries has made it easier for managers to lower their account size minimums, thereby making it easier for a Standards Director to access good managers on a separate account basis.

However, just because a portfolio meets the minimum account size requirement for a particular money manager doesn't mean that a separate account is the best vehicle for the portfolio. For this reason, we provide an outline of some of the pros and cons for each of the different types of investment vehicles so that an appropriate choice can be made.

* **Costs:** Mutual funds spread their costs across all shareholders— a good thing if a wealth holder has a small investment in the mutual fund; a potentially bad thing if the wealth holder has a large investment. Also, the Standards Director may be able to negotiate lower fees with a separate account manager; in some jurisdictions, regulations prohibit mutual funds from such negotiations.
* **Audits:** In some jurisdictions, mutual funds are required to be audited by independent accounting firms. In most jurisdictions, separate account managers are only encouraged to have their performance audited.
* **Performance information:** Despite advances in technology, mutual fund databases are still a bit more reliable; in addition, performance information is reported sooner than separate account data and probably always will be. The mutual fund only needs to calculate the performance of only one portfolio, whereas the separate account manager needs to calculate performance across a wide range of portfolios.
* **Tax management:** The taxable portfolio, particularly one with low-basis stock, will likely fare better with a separate account manager that is willing, and has the ability, to provide a tax-sensitive investment strategy.

♦ **Fund liquidations and purchases:** The mutual fund manager is disadvantaged in that the manager must also contend with purchases and liquidations within the fund. This can be a major problem in a down market when the investing herd tries to move out of a fund, forcing the manager to sell securities against the better judgment of the manager.

♦ **Diversification:** Generally speaking, mutual funds tend to be more diversified than separate account managers. For this reason, if the wealth holder is willing to accept more volatility, he or she may prefer a concentrated, separately managed account.

♦ **Specific identification of securities:** Some wealth holders prefer seeing "their" portfolio as opposed to being invested with the masses.

ESSENTIAL LEADERSHIP BEHAVIOR: DISCIPLINED

Defined as: Showing self-restraint; regimented; driven; high endurance; committed; sets appropriate pace for self and staff

A Standards Director who has strong "disciplined" skills has a tendency to:

♦ Show the capacity to work rapidly and efficiently
♦ Provide subordinates with the authority to decide and act within areas of assigned duties
♦ Clarify for staff the priority of an assignment relative to other assignments

A Standards Director who has weak "disciplined" skills has a tendency to:

♦ Give insufficient information or explanation when assigning tasks
♦ Perceive staff as lacking in competence and believe no one else can be as effective and efficient in completing an assignment
♦ Fear a loss of control and prefer a strong, hands-on approach
♦ Abdicate responsibility for a final result to others and assume they will follow through without a system in place to check progress and results

Dimension 4.3: Ensure that service agreements and contracts do not contain provisions that conflict with objectives

Leadership Behavior: Fair-minded

Standard

The Standards Director ensures that service agreements and contracts with money managers and service providers do not contain provisions that conflict with the wealth holder's goals and objectives.

> Blind trust alone should not provide comfort in wealth management any more than in air travel. But the industry of wealth management exalts trust; it does not demand process and discipline of its clients because discipline and process would remove the sense of complexity and powerlessness that requires customers to pay so much for so little. People trusted Madoff, Lehman, Weavering, AIG, and so on. Trustworthiness is the garb of the scoundrel who can sell his fraud, so long as he is clothed with trust.
>
> —Chapter 4

The purpose of this dimension is to ensure that money managers and other service providers understand the role they are intended to play and the performance objectives or conditions that must be met to achieve that purpose. Successful implementation of a wealth management strategy is a combination of rigorous process and execution, and like any other worthy endeavor, no job is complete until the paperwork is done!

The review of contracts and agreements is an important additional step to ensure that there are no misunderstandings between the roles and responsibilities of all parties involved in the wealth management strategy. Our suggestions regarding the review of contracts and agreements are very general in nature, and again we need to caution the Standards Director to discuss legal matters with a knowledgeable attorney.

* Define the scope of the relationship.
* Refer to regulations or trust documents that establish the legal character of a portfolio and may define or limit certain investment practices.
* Refer to documents that govern the investment strategy (such as a PWPS), particularly documents that define performance criteria.

A good practice is to periodically review contracts and service agreements to ensure that the wealth management strategy still requires the contracted services and that the money manager's or service provider's pricing is still competitive; or to discover new services the service provider may be able to provide the wealth management program.

ESSENTIAL LEADERSHIP BEHAVIOR: FAIR-MINDED

Defined as: Sensitive; just and impartial; values diversity; empathetic; strong interpersonal skills (high emotional intelligence); persuasive

A Standards Director who has strong "fair-minded" skills has a tendency to:

+ Accept people at face value without filtering their words or actions through personal biases
+ Embrace values without imposing them on others
+ Accept different viewpoints without judgment
+ Try to find common ground with others rather than focus on dissimilarities

A Standards Director who has weak "fair-minded" skills has a tendency to:

+ Respond more favorably to those individuals who share his or her views, background, or values
+ Become locked into his or her own viewpoint and be resistant to change
+ Fail to distinguish how people differ from one another and see only that they differ from the Director

20

Step 5: Monitor

Building strategies and following processes, executing the vision of what wealth is for, requires expertise that many wealth holders do not have as well as considerable time and attention that many wealth holders do not want to devote. The management of significant family wealth, like any worthwhile enterprise, requires standards to govern operations, to measure performance, to ensure proper process, and ultimately to avoid disasters like Madoff, Stanford, and others. A wealth holder wanting to live life free from the burdens of wealth will want to delegate the management of wealth but will require accountability and measurement tools to ensure that the wealth is being managed appropriately.

—Chapter 12

Once the optimal wealth management strategy has been designed, the PWPS prepared, and the strategy implemented, the final critical step is the ongoing monitoring and assessment of the wealth management program. Monitoring the resulting performance of selected service providers and evaluating the continuing viability of the wealth holder's goals and objectives constitutes the next-to-final step of the wealth management process.

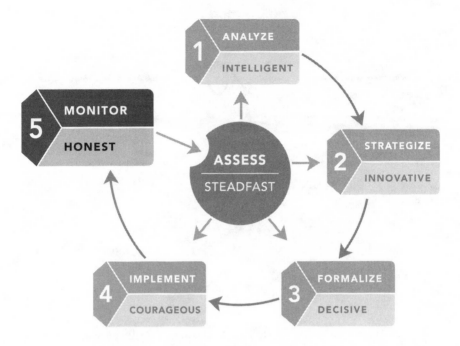

The monitoring function extends beyond a strict examination of performance: by definition, monitoring occurs across all policy and procedural issues. Monitoring includes an analysis of not only what happened but also why.

Step 5: MONITOR	HONEST
Decision-Making Dimensions	**Leadership Behaviors**
5.1: Prepare periodic reports that compare performance with objectives.	*Diligent*
5.2: Prepare periodic reports that analyze costs or ROI, with performance and objectives.	*Accountable*
5.3: Perform periodic examinations for conflicts-of-interest and self-dealing, and breaches of a code of conduct.	*Genuine*
5.4: Prepare periodic qualitative or performance reviews of decision makers.	*Motivational*

ESSENTIAL LEADERSHIP BEHAVIOR: HONEST

Defined as: Marked by integrity; reputable; moral

The measurement of honesty defies the abilities of social research. Sociologists say that a person can be honest all his or her life and then confront a situation in which he or she lacks the courage to do the right thing (hence the link to the preceding leadership behavior—courage).

Dimension 5.1: Prepare periodic reports that compare performance with objectives

Leadership Behavior: Diligent

5 MONITOR

HONEST

Standard

The Standards Director defines a process to periodically monitor the wealth management strategy to ensure that it is meeting defined goals and objectives.

The board of a well-run company always has its expectations for job performance articulated and its review procedures well developed. Worldwide, family office executives bemoan the fact that their "constituents" do not appreciate how well they do their jobs. Of course, some constituents actually do understand the efforts and skill it takes but not all. And more than one family office executive has taken advantage of his or her position to defraud the family.

—Chapter 12

The preparation and maintenance of the PWPS is the most critical function the Standards Director performs. The second most critical function is monitoring. This is the step where the Standards Director will likely make the most mistakes and, even when executed properly, will be the costliest component of the wealth management program—in terms of time, the staff required, and the technology to be employed.

When done properly, monitoring triggers a number of periodic reviews:

- **Monthly:** At least monthly, the Standards Director should analyze custodial statements. He or she should pay particular attention to transactions initiated by separate account managers: (1) Are the trades consistent with the manager's stated strategy, and (2) is there evidence that the manager is seeking best price and execution (Dimension 5.2)?
- **Quarterly:** At least quarterly, the Standards Director should compare:
  - The wealth holder's actual asset allocation to the strategic asset allocation defined in the PWPS to determine whether the portfolio should be rebalanced back to the strategic asset allocation (Dimension 3.1). The discipline of rebalancing, in essence, controls risk and forces the wealth strategy to move along a predetermined path. Rebalancing limits should be set so they do not trigger continuous readjustment to the portfolio—we have found that a collar of plus or minus 5 percent around the strategic asset allocation works fine.

- ◆ Money manager performance against benchmarks established in the PWPS, including a comparison of each manager's performance against an appropriate index and peer group.
- ◆ **Annually:** At least annually, there should be a formal review of the PWPS to determine whether the wealth holder's goals and objectives have changed and whether the wealth management strategy still holds the highest probability of meeting stated goals and objectives.

Central to the monitoring function is *performance attribution analysis*, which consists of two overlapping and sequential procedures: (1) performance measurement, the science; and (2) performance evaluation, the art.

Performance measurement consists of calculating portfolio statistics (standard deviation; Alpha, Sharpe, and Sortino ratios) and rates of return. Although performance measurement is referred to as the "science," it is far from being exact.

The source and handling of the data used in performance measurement may have an impact on calculations. For this reason, the Standards Director should request performance information from different sources to try to catch potential errors. For example, the rate of return calculated by the custodian may differ from the rate of return reported by a money manager, and both of these returns may yet be different from the rate of return the Director calculates using the Director's own performance measurement software. Like navigating a ship at sea, the prudent sailor takes as many bearings as possible to try to triangulate an exact fix.

Performance evaluation is where the skills of the Standards Director come into play: other decision makers will be looking to the Director to identify the appropriate call to action. It is this phase of the analysis where the Director compares the results of performance measurement to the portfolio's PWPS and, if needed, suggest appropriate action to bring the wealth management strategy back into alignment.

+ What is the current asset allocation of the overall portfolio?
+ Does it need to be rebalanced? If so, what are the cash flows for the coming six months, and can these cash flows (contributions or disbursements) be used to rebalance the portfolio?
+ How has each money manager performed relative to their indices and peer groups? Is there evidence that a money manager may be deviating from the stated strategy?
+ Are there managers that should be placed on a watch list or even terminated?

The decision to terminate a manager should not be taken lightly, since there are a number of costs associated with changing managers. When poor performance becomes an issue, it is important that the Standards Director approach the evaluation process with the same rigor he or she applied when conducting due diligence on the money manager. In fact, we suggest it is prudent to apply the same due diligence criteria that the Director used in the search phase (Step 4):

+ Has there been a change to the portfolio team?
+ Has the money manager encountered legal or regulatory problems?
+ Has there been a change in the money manager's strategy?
+ Has there been a change in the asset allocation structure of the money manager's portfolio (for example, is the manager beginning to hold more cash)?
+ Has there been a marked increase in portfolio turnover?
+ Has the money manager consistently performed below the returns of an appropriate index or below the manager's peer group?
+ Has risk-adjusted performance (Alpha, Sharpe, and Sortino ratios) dropped below the performance of an appropriate index or below the money manager's peer group?

Over the years, we have seen a lot of wealth managers try to quantify when a money manager should be terminated—for example, a certain number of quarters below a benchmark. We think a disciplined methodology is essential; however, the best approach is remarkably simple: *Fire the manager when you have lost confidence in his or her ability to do the job.*

What we say here for money managers is just as true for other advisors and employees. If expectations are clearly articulated by the Standards Director, the performance of every accountant, every lawyer, every advisor, and every employee must be evaluated regularly in terms of those expectations. Any should be fired when you lose confidence in his or her ability to do that job.

ESSENTIAL LEADERSHIP BEHAVIOR: DILIGENT

Defined as: Steady; earnest; energetic; stays on task

A Standards Director who has strong "diligent" skills has a tendency to:

◆ Judge output by internal standards and not simply the performance levels of others
◆ Sustain an effort that is methodical and consistent, keeping the wealth holder's goals and objectives in sight
◆ Not permit sloppy or careless effort regardless of how a task is ranked in importance
◆ Focus on the quantitative measure of results produced, whether engaged in a repetitive, singular activity or frequently changing and diverse tasks

A Standards Director who has weak "diligent" skills has a tendency to:

◆ Find it difficult to tune out or defer distractions that draw time and attention away from the task at hand
◆ Be selective to the attention of detail, disregarding or delegating what the wealth manager does not consider crucial to the accomplishment of goals
◆ Easily lose interest in results-oriented activities (monitoring) in favor of more satisfying opportunities offered in the arenas of personal relationships
◆ Be casual or informal about tracking the progress of goals and objectives

Dimension 5.2: Prepare periodic reports that analyze costs, or return on investment, with performance and objectives

Leadership Behavior: Accountable

5 MONITOR

HONEST

Standard

The Standards Director periodically analyzes all fees and expenses associated with the wealth management strategy, including:

a. Fees paid to money managers, custodians, and investment consultants
b. Brokerage costs and use of soft dollars
c. Fees and expenses of service providers

Measuring costs requires identifying what is paid to the provider but also what is paid or lost to poor advice. The fee paid the most expensive estate planner for the most sophisticated family limited partnership pales beside the loss in value and freedom suffered when that partnership is imposed on the dysfunctional family and becomes cannon fodder for their pitched battles.

No matter what the business, decision makers have a responsibility to control and account for expenses. The Standards Director's role is no exception.

Wealth management costs and expenses can be broken down into four broad categories. Certain expenses can be obscured or moved from one category to another to create apparent savings, so Standards Directors are cautioned to consider costs across all four categories.

♦ **Advisor fees, employee salaries, and money manager fees and expenses:** These comparisons should be made by peer group or investment strategy. For example, the Standards Director should not compare the fees of a large-cap manager to those of a small-cap manager. The Director also should watch the fees being paid for alternative investment strategies: The differences between traditional money management and hedge fund strategies have begun to blur, yet the costs associated with hedge funds are considerably higher. Why pay many times more for an investment strategy that is largely accomplished by a traditional money manager with lower fees and expenses?

- **Trading costs for separately managed portfolios, including commission charges (soft dollars) and execution expenses (best execution):** This large and important component of cost control is often overlooked and can be the subject of abuse if not carefully monitored. A simple check the Standards Director can employ is to analyze the custodial statement and see which brokerage firms are being used by the separate account manager to trade the portfolio's account. (If that level of detail is not being provided by the custodian, the Director may want to consider changing custodians or request the trading information directly from the money manager.) Ideally, the Director wants to see that the money manager is using a host of different brokerage firms for executing the trades and that commission charges are in the institutional range (in the United States, 4 to 8 cents per share). If that is not evident, a call to the money manager is warranted for an explanation.

- **Custodial charges, including custodial fees, transaction charges, and cash management fees:** As noted in Dimension 4.1, the Standards Director should check the expense ratio of the money market fund being used by the custodian to ensure that the cash accounts are invested in an institutional money market.

- **Consulting, recordkeeping, or administrative costs and fees:** Particular attention should be paid to determine whether there are revenue-sharing or finder's fee arrangements between service providers. If such fees exist, they should be applied to the benefit of the wealth holder.

The Standards Director has the responsibility to identify every party that has been compensated from the wealth holder's portfolio and demonstrate that the compensation received by every money manager and service provider was fair and reasonable for the level of services being provided.

The Standards Director is also accountable for ensuring that each provider has what is needed to perform services well and efficiently.

ESSENTIAL LEADERSHIP BEHAVIOR: ACCOUNTABLE

Defined as: Takes responsibility; dependable; budget–cost–ROI conscious

A Standards Director who has strong "accountable" skills has a tendency to:

- Make optimal use of available resources and personnel
- Be disciplined in collecting and analyzing key performance measures
- Have a realistic grasp of financials, show responsiveness to the need for economies and cost control, and be able to draw meaningful implications from financial data
- Focus on approaches and techniques designed to increase production or decrease costs, enhancing overall profitability

A Standards Director who has weak "accountable" skills has a tendency to:

- Make excuses for poor performance or publicly blame others
- Not find the time or justify the effort to establish and review financial controls
- Fail to implement steps to monitor key financial or wealth holder data that can potentially impact bottom-line profitability
- Become distracted from the goal of profitability by "squeaky wheel" situations

Dimension 5.3: Conduct periodic examinations for conflicts of interest, self-dealing, and breaches of a code of conduct

MONITOR

5

HONEST

Leadership Behavior: Genuine

Standard

The Standards Director periodically reviews compensation agreements and service agreements of service providers to ensure that they do not contain provisions that:

a. Conflict with the wealth holder's goals and objectives
b. Are performance-based using short- to intermediate-term (less than five years) investment results

The Standards Director also defines in writing an ethics statement and periodically checks for conflicts of interest. The ethics statement requires all persons involved with managing wealth to:

a. Annually acknowledge the ethics statement
b. Disclose all conflicts of interest as they become known

Distrust and fear are impediments to comfort. Lack of control or understanding can create anxiety and discomfort. What you do not know or understand makes you uncomfortable because it is hard to relax in the presence of uncertainty and threats unseen.

—Chapter 4

The most common mistake made by service providers is the omission of one or more prudent practices, as opposed to the commission of a prohibited act or being involved in a conflict of interest. However, instances of the latter are common enough that the Standards Director should monitor the wealth management program for possible problems. Any activity that is not in the best interest of the wealth holder will cause problems, and it is critical that the Director ensure that no party has been unduly enriched by the wealth holder's assets.

Paraphrasing Stephen M. R. Covey from his bestseller, *The Speed of Trust*, "trust" has become the global currency for the wealth management industry. Trust has to be the basis for every relationship the wealth holder has with service providers, particularly the relationship with the Standards Director. It is the Standards Director who is responsible for *setting the tone at the top*; the ethical standards defined and exhibited by the Director cannot be underestimated. The behavior of the wealth management team oftentimes will mirror the standards of integrity and fair dealing (i.e., avoidance of conflicts of interests and self-entitlements) exhibited by the Director.

With trust comes the duty of loyalty; no one involved in managing the wealth holder's assets should invest or manage portfolio assets in such a way that there arises even a hint of a personal conflict of interest. Decision makers have a duty to employ an objective, independent due diligence process at all times and have defined policies and procedures to manage potential conflicts of interests.

The Difference Between a Code of Conduct and a Code of Ethics

A code of conduct, by definition, is rules-based. In contrast, a code of ethics is principles-based; at least, it should be. Unfortunately, most of the ethical codes we see written for the wealth management industry are rules-based and compliance-driven; therefore, they should be labeled codes of conduct.

The distinction is important because rules-based conduct rarely succeeds over the long term. Rules rarely elicit as high a level of behavior as principles: rules require little discernment, whereas principles require a full engagement of the head and the heart.

When drafting or reviewing codes of conduct or ethical codes, the Standards Director should remember that rules often weaken original intent. Principles require more work—in drafting and in explaining to those affected—but, in the long term, principles will have a more positive impact on the wealth management program.

Performance-Based Fees

Some money managers and family office staff prefer performance-based fee arrangements. Under these terms, the money manager or staff member receives a higher compensation if he or she is able to exceed a predetermined performance benchmark over a specified period. The argument for these arrangements is that it puts the money manager and staff member on the same side of the table as the wealth holder: *If I make more money for the wealth holder, I should make more money.*

Unfortunately, it has been demonstrated time and again that such arrangements may not be in the wealth holder's best interest. If performance is lagging the predetermined benchmark, there is a tendency for decision makers to "double-down," or increase the level of portfolio risk, in order to make up for lagging performance. Often, the portfolio becomes highly concentrated in "sure bets," leaving the wealth holder undiversified. If performance-based fees are to be permitted, the risks associated with such fees should be mitigated by extending the specified performance period to five years or more. This way decision makers are still incentivized to manage assets with a long-term perspective.

Hourly fees must be considered carefully as they can incentivize inefficiency by rewarding the provider if the work takes a long time and employs many people. What is more valuable, having your work done well and promptly or well and slowly and inefficiently?

ESSENTIAL LEADERSHIP BEHAVIOR: GENUINE

Defined as: Sincere and honest; free from pretense; supportive

A Standards Director who has strong "genuine" skills has a tendency to:

- Present factual information without embellishment or bias
- Build a reputation as a credible resource
- Take pride in being a role model

A Standards Director who has weak "genuine" skills has a tendency to:

- Color information by filtering it through his or her own biases
- Lose patience with individuals lacking the same motivation or enthusiasm as his or her own
- Withhold advice or support until it is expressly requested by others
- Resist being obligated to function in an advisory capacity

Dimension 5.4: Prepare periodic qualitative reviews or performance reviews of decision makers

Leadership Behavior: Motivational

5 MONITOR

HONEST

Standard

The Standards Director prepares periodic qualitative reviews of money managers and service providers.

What is wealth for? We find universal and global agreement that it is not to cause unhappiness. It is not to create fiduciary burdens. It is not to enslave in governance structures. It is not to be weighed down with responsibilities. Freedom from wealth, getting on with life, self-actualization—all have to be possible in whatever design is created to make the wealth do what it is for. Gaining freedom from the burdens of wealth requires wisdom and process—wisdom to allow perspective and process to allow delegation of the minutiae. Together those can provide comfort to lead life free of the burdens of wealth.

—Chapter 2

The Standards Director's review of a service provider needs to extend beyond an examination of the provider's past performance.

Providers of services to private wealth holders are organic, constantly evolving, and subject to the same challenges that every other organization faces—managing people. Disturbances in the workplace will eventually be reflected in performance. Conversely, as we witnessed with certain firms caught up in the U.S. mutual fund scandals of 2003, a decline in investment performance may lure senior investment professionals to compromise principles and permit practices that conflict with the best interests of their portfolios.

Even money management firms that state that they rely on a quantitative model (black box) still need professionals to interpret and implement the output. For this reason, the Standards Director needs to periodically assess the qualitative factors of hired money managers. Although not true in every case, or every geographic locale, there are some general observations we can make about the qualitative factors that affect the wealth management industry:

♦ **Ownership:** Decision makers who are owners of their firms tend to outperform those who are employees.
♦ **Size of the firm:** Smaller organizations tend to be more focused and concentrated in one style. As a result, performance tends to be more volatile—they bounce between the top of the performance universe and sometimes the bottom.
♦ **Assets under management:** This is a close corollary to the size of the firm. The Standards Director should ensure that the firm can properly invest the dollars being placed, which will vary

depending on the asset class. The manager fulfilling a large-cap equity assignment can effectively manage larger amounts than a small-cap manager.

+ **Change in personnel:** When there has been a change in personnel, or when a decision maker has left one firm to join another, prudence dictates that the firm be placed on hold until sufficient time (e.g., two years) has passed in order to determine the impact the change may have on performance.

+ **Trading capability:** Execution costs have a great impact on performance (Dimension 5.2). The Standards Director should inquire about the firm's in-house trading capability, as well as how the firm ensures the portfolio is receiving favorable or best execution of trades.

+ **Research:** The research analysts often are the unsung heroes: they're the ones reading the fine print of annual reports and bond indentures to find the gold nuggets for the portfolio managers. How a firm treats, and values, its research analysts will say a lot about the firm. The Standards Director asking the simple question "what percentage of your research is purchased from the street?" will give the Director a good insight into the qualitative decision-making process of the firm. A firm that is relying heavily on research bought from the "street" (that is, from third-party vendors) is going to have difficulty outperforming other managers who are looking at the same data.

+ **Soft dollars:** Managers who purchase "street" research usually pay for the information from commissions generated from portfolio transactions. Under such a scenario, the Standards Director should understand that part of the manager's costs for running the organization is paid for by transactions generated from the wealth holder's portfolio.

+ **Conflicts policies:** The conflicts policies of lawyers, accountants, advisors, and money managers should be studied, and the Standards Director should understand exactly what they are and how they apply to the wealth holder's situation.

ESSENTIAL LEADERSHIP BEHAVIOR: MOTIVATIONAL

Defined as: Ability to persuade others to take positive action; committed to the success of the organization and the well-being of staff and portfolios

A Standards Director who has strong "motivational" skills has a tendency to:

* Elicit cooperation through persuasion rather than authority
* Earn respect rather than demand it
* Develop champions who are capable of acting self-sufficiently
* Run interference and fight for resources for staff
* Eliminate irrelevant issues that will cloud the objectives

A Standards Director who has weak "motivational" skills has a tendency to:

* Assume that all staff share the same goals as the Director
* Not step into the role of being a potential catalyst for a team effort
* Rely on the authority of the Director's position and title to influence others
* Lose power by expecting subordinates to commit to more objectives than they can handle

21

Assessment Procedures

"Family legacy and values" sounds eloquent, and the phrase has become the clarion opening of many family wealth conversations. "Legacy" takes us together as a family through history, and "values" bind us forevermore. Those words give perpetuity to the family just as trusts now give perpetuity to the wealth.

But though the words roll out with grandeur, the pragmatics of designing family legacy and embracing family values are difficult. Indeed the road to functionality is strewn with the carcasses of legacies and values.

—Chapter 10

The final element of a procedurally prudent wealth management program is assessing whether the process is effective.

A long-term wealth management strategy requires alternation only when the underlying factors of the wealth holder's goals and objectives change. These changes tend to be infrequent, if not rare, and reviews directed toward constantly reassessing existing strategy and policy tend to be counterproductive. The Standards Director should be particularly cautious of making changes during periods of market extremes.

Despite the infrequent need for policy modifications, periodic reviews can serve a very productive purpose. When aimed at educating other decision makers or family members, reviews can reinforce the logic for current policy and therefore reduce the chances of unnecessary alterations. In addition, whenever significant events occur that warrant a review, the Standards Director should ensure that the wealth management strategy is examined in an orderly fashion.

Whether the Standards Director is helping the wealth holder to define goals and objectives, developing the investment strategy, or implementing and monitoring the strategy, the success of the wealth management program will be determined by the quality of the Director's decision-making process. For that reason the Director also should develop effective assessment procedures to evaluate the strengths and weaknesses of his or her own decision-making process and also to assess his or her effectiveness as the leader of that process.

There are numerous benefits to having a defined assessment process:

- ◆ It demonstrates to the wealth holder, family members, and other decision makers that the Standards Director has a procedurally prudent wealth management process in place.
- ◆ The assessment process can double as a training curriculum for educating other decision makers and family members.
- ◆ It may help the Standards Director and/or the wealth holder to discover blind spots—shortfalls and omissions to the wealth management process.
- ◆ It can facilitate the sharing of best practices with other Standards Directors.
- ◆ It can help improve the wealth management process—an objective worthy of all of our efforts.

We have prepared an assessment instrument for Standards Directors that is based on the decision-making dimensions and leadership behaviors covered in this book. The assessment instrument will help Directors gain a better understanding of their own strengths and weaknesses so that they have a basis for considering additional professional development.

In closing, the intelligent and prudent management of a wealth management strategy requires that the Standards Director maintain a rational, consistent investment process. The Director can accomplish the lion's share of the wealth holder's goals and objectives by implementing a simple decision-making process, such as the one defined in this book.

ESSENTIAL LEADERSHIP BEHAVIOR: STEADFAST

Defined as: Focused on achieving goals and objectives; efficient; practical; capacity to balance the needs of the organization and portfolio

A Standards Director who has strong "steadfast" skills has a tendency to:

+ Put the interests of the wealth holder first
+ Deliver promised results to the wealth holder without unnecessary fanfare or embellishment
+ Look for ways to improve

A Standards Director who has weak "steadfast" skills has a tendency to:

+ Focus more on style and making a good impression than content and relevance
+ Revise commitments when faced with unanticipated barriers
+ View "not failing" as an acceptable measure of achievement

Self-Assessment Instrument for Standards Directors

Instructions: This assessment instrument is designed to help you, the Standards Director, evaluate a wealth management process against a defined ethos. For each statement, indicate whether it represents a strength (1), a weakness (4), or an area that needs some improvement (2 or 3). As with any self-assessment, the purpose of this exercise is to help you identify the strengths and weaknesses within your wealth management program. Reviewing your responses will assist you in both identifying the areas in the process you may have overlooked and communicating your needs to other professionals and family members.

		Dimension	Strength—Weakness			
1	The wealth holder's goals and objectives are clearly stated.	1.1	**1**	**2**	**3**	**4**
2	You use a deliberative process to help develop the wealth holder's goals and objectives.	1.1	**1**	**2**	**3**	**4**
3	The wealth holder's goals and objectives are consistent with applicable regulations, statutes, and established policies and procedures.	1.1	**1**	**2**	**3**	**4**
4	Documents that substantiate the wealth holder's goals and objectives are centrally filed.	1.1	**1**	**2**	**3**	**4**
5	You ensure other decision makers understand their roles and responsibilities.	1.2	**1**	**2**	**3**	**4**
6	You have an understanding of the standards, procedures, policies, rules, and regulations that affect the wealth management strategy.	1.3	**1**	**2**	**3**	**4**
7	You ensure that the wealth holder is tax compliant (complying with appropriate standards).	1.3	**1**	**2**	**3**	**4**
8	When you lack expertise, you delegate to experts who have been prudently selected.	1.3	**1**	**2**	**3**	**4**
9	The experts who have been prudently selected are monitored.	1.3	**1**	**2**	**3**	**4**
10	You understand the risks associated with the wealth management strategy.	2.1	**1**	**2**	**3**	**4**

		Dimension	Strength—Weakness			
11	You are circumspect in planning and action to mitigate or manage risks.	2.1	1	2	3	4
12	You have the capacity to bear uncertainty (risk) with fortitude and calm.	2.1	1	2	3	4
13	You have identified the appropriate asset classes for the wealth management strategy.	2.2	1	2	3	4
14	You have identified the investment time horizon associated with the goals and objectives of the wealth management strategy.	2.3	1	2	3	4
15	You have defined the short-term, tactical performance objectives of the wealth management strategy.	2.4	1	2	3	4
16	The wealth management strategy is consistent with the risk tolerances, asset class preferences, time horizon, and expected outcomes of the investment program.	3.1	1	2	3	4
17	You ensure that there are appropriate liquid assets to meet near-term obligations.	3.2	1	2	3	4
18	The wealth management strategy is consistent with your implementation and monitoring constraints.	3.2	1	2	3	4
19	You have prepared the PWPS.	3.3	1	2	3	4
20	The PWPS has sufficient detail that a "competent stranger" can execute with confidence.	3.3	1	2	3	4

		Dimension	Strength—Weakness			
21	The PWPS has been reviewed and approved by the wealth holder.	3.3	1	2	3	4
22	You have a detailed due diligence process for selecting money managers.	4.1	1	2	3	4
23	You can demonstrate that the due diligence process has been consistently applied.	4.1	1	2	3	4
24	You have a due diligence process for evaluating the custodian.	4.1	1	2	3	4
25	You have considered the pros and cons of active and passive managers and have appropriately implemented the wealth management strategy.	4.2	1	2	3	4
26	You have considered the pros and cons of separate account managers and mutual funds (commingled trusts) and have appropriately implemented the wealth management strategy.	4.2	1	2	3	4
27	Agreements of substance with service vendors are in writing, and they define the scope and expectations, and are consistent with, the wealth holder's goals and objectives.	4.3	1	2	3	4
28	You have a system in place to periodically monitor and evaluate whether the wealth management strategy will meet the wealth holder's goals and objectives.	5.1	1	2	3	4
29	You look beyond performance returns to analyze whether the wealth holder's goals and objectives are being met.	5.1	1	2	3	4

		Dimension	Strength—Weakness			
30	There is a defined process for determining when a money manager should be terminated, and the process is consistently applied.	5.1	1	2	3	4
31	You control and account for investment expenses.	5.2	1	2	3	4
32	When employing separate account managers, you ensure that each manager is seeking best execution and is appropriately applying soft dollars.	5.2	1	2	3	4
33	You avoid conflicts of interest.	5.3	1	2	3	4
34	You make periodic investigations into possible conflicts of interest of other decision makers.	5.3	1	2	3	4
35	You conduct periodic qualitative reviews of money managers.	5.4	1	2	3	4
36	You have a process in place to periodically assess the overall effectiveness of the wealth management strategy.	5.4	1	2	3	4

APPENDIX

Sample Private Wealth Policy Statement (PWPS)

THIS PWPS IS INTENDED TO SERVE AS AN OUTLINE AND FRAMEwork for a procedurally prudent wealth management process. Each section should be customized to the wealth holder's specific goals, objectives, and unique circumstances.

Contents

Section I: Definitions
Section II: Purpose
Section III: Statement of Principles
Section IV: Duties and Responsibilities
Section V: Ethics Statement
Section VI: Persons Serving in a Fiduciary Capacity
Section VII: Inputs Used to Develop the Wealth Management Strategy
Section VIII: Money Manager and Custodian
Section IX: Monitoring Procedures
Section X: Review of the PWPS

Section I: Definitions

Whenever used in the PWPS, the following terms have the intended meaning:

Money manager is inclusive of separate account managers, mutual funds, commingled trusts, and hedge fund managers.

Service provider(s) is inclusive of family office staff, attorneys, accountants, money managers, investment consultants, custodians, and any other key advisors providing wealth management services.

Standards Director is the representative appointed by the wealth holder who is responsible for the management of the wealth holder's goals and objectives in accordance with the Principles and the Standards. It is expected that the Standards Director will prudently delegate whenever he or she lacks expertise, or capacity, in a particular Standard.

Wealth holder is an individual of wealth; trustees of a trust; directors or trustees of an eleemosynary (foundation, operating charity, or endowment) or corporation (partnership); or any person holding substantial wealth as a legal owner under the laws of the jurisdiction involved.

Section II: Purpose

The purpose of this PWPS is to guide the Standards Director in the development, implementation, and monitoring of the wealth holder's wealth management strategy by:

1. Stating the wealth holder's attitudes, expectations, objectives, and guidelines for the management of wealth
2. Setting forth an investment structure for managing the wealth that includes various asset classes and money management styles that, in total, are expected to produce an appropriate level of diversification and a sufficient investment return
3. Providing guidelines that control the level of risk and liquidity, consistent with stated objectives

4. Encouraging effective communications between the wealth holder, Standards Director, and service providers
5. Establishing formal criteria to monitor, evaluate, and assess all sections of this PWPS

Section III: Statement of Principles

This PWPS has been arrived at on consideration of the following Principles, which have been adopted by the wealth holder:

1. The wealth holder, the trustees of a trust, or the directors of a foundation shall articulate purposes, goals, objectives, expectations, and risk tolerance with respect to the wealth and shall be ultimately responsible for maintaining the currency of that articulation.
2. With respect to a family office, a trust, or a foundation, the governance structure together with various governance roles and responsibilities shall be clearly set forth and shall include provision for the communication of those roles and responsibilities and assurance that they are understood and accepted.
3. Any trust or foundation and any trustee or director shall adhere to best fiduciary practices, and there shall be established process for monitoring the discharge of fiduciary duties by the trust, the foundation, a trustee, or a director.
4. Succession shall be set out where possible and shall be considered. For the wealth holder provisions shall be in existence for disposition of assets and management of affairs from and after death or in the event of incapacity. For the family office, trust, or foundation, provision shall be made for succession of governance and management.
5. Each investment portfolio shall be diversified as completely as is practical. There should be diversification of asset classes, investment managers, investment style, currencies, banking and brokerage exposure, and geopolitical risks.
6. Every portfolio shall have an investment policy statement, and every manager shall have a clearly articulated mandate; the investment policy statement and mandate shall be monitored.

7. Any investment portfolio shall be designed taking into account the assets, objectives, needs, and character of the owner and/or beneficiary and shall be monitored with those in mind. A foundation shall have a process to determine whether the investment program reflects the values of its mission and its philanthropic grant program.

8. There shall be clear, disciplined, and objective processes for selecting, monitoring, removing, and replacing investment managers, custodians, banks, and trade execution, accounting, and other professionals.

9. Any investment manager or specific fund to be used shall have a strategy and style that can be easily understood and explained to others by the wealth holder or by one of the trustees, directors, or staff members of the trust, foundation, or family office. If no one other than the investment manager or the fund representative is able to explain the strategy and style, the manager or fund shall not be used.

10. Special scrutiny and limitations should be applied to any investment manager who does not provide complete transparency or whose portfolio is not liquid; such investments are not prohibited but should be limited in proportion to total portfolio investments.

11. Custody of assets, accounting for assets, and investment management services shall each be performed independently and separately.

12. There shall be an established process for managing and monitoring internal and external resources.

13. There shall be full transparency of fees and expenses.

14. Compensation and fees paid to staff, directors, and governors of family offices, foundations, or boards shall not be calculated on the basis of investment return of shorter duration than five years. Any salary, bonus, or fee must be fully disclosed as to its amount and its calculation. Any direct or indirect payment to or for staff or governors other than a payment designated salary, bonus, or fee (or similar designation) is prohibited.

15. Self-dealing by staff, trustees, or directors of any family office, trust, or foundation is strictly prohibited. Investment portfolios of those parties shall be subject to strict disclosure rules that

assure compliance with the prohibition against self-dealing. Any grant or payment to any agency or company in which such a party has any interest whatsoever should clearly reflect that interest in the deliberation relating to that grant or payment.

Section IV: Duties and Responsibilities

To ensure alignment that all parties involved in the decision-making process are in sync, each party's role and responsibilities shall be communicated in writing.

Wealth Holder's Role

It is the responsibility of the wealth holder to communicate to the Standards Director any changes to the wealth holder's goals and objectives that may materially impact the management of this PWPS. Furthermore, it is the responsibility of the wealth holder to communicate stated goals and objectives to other family members and to associates as appropriate.

Standards Director's Role

The Standards Director is the representative appointed by the wealth holder to be responsible for the development, implementation, and monitoring of the wealth management strategy. The Standards Director is authorized, if not highly encouraged, to delegate sections of this PWPS to prudent experts when the Standards Director lacks such expertise or capacity.

Money Managers

The specific duties and responsibilities of each money manager are:

1. Manage the assets under its supervision in accordance with the guidelines and objectives outlined in respective service agreements, prospectuses, or trust agreements.
2. Exercise full investment discretion with regards to buying, managing, and selling assets held in the portfolio.
3. If managing a separate account (as opposed to a mutual fund, hedge fund, or commingled trust), seek approval from the

Standards Director prior to purchasing and/or implementing the following securities and transactions:

   a. Letter stock and other unregistered securities; commodities or other commodity contracts; and short sales or margin transactions

   b. Securities lending; and pledging or hypothecating securities

   c. Investments for the purpose of exercising control of management

   d. Illiquid securities

4. Provide the Standards Director, upon request, a listing of all securities (unless managing a mutual fund or a commingled trust).

5. Vote promptly all proxies and related actions in a manner consistent with the long-term interest and objectives of the wealth as described in this PWPS; each money manager shall keep detailed records of the voting of proxies and related actions and comply with all applicable regulatory obligations.

6. Communicate to the Standards Director all significant changes pertaining to the portfolio it manages or the firm itself; changes in ownership, organizational structure, financial condition, and professional staff are examples of changes to the firm in which the Standards Director is interested.

7. Effect all transactions for the portfolio subject to best price and execution; if the money manager utilizes brokerage from the account's assets to effect soft dollar transactions, detailed records will be kept and communicated to the Standards Director.

8. Use the same care, skill, prudence, and due diligence under the circumstances then prevailing that experienced investment professionals would use, and in accordance and compliance with all applicable laws, rules, and regulations.

Custodian

Custodians are responsible for the safekeeping of the wealth. The specific duties and responsibilities of the custodian are:

1. Maintain separate accounts by legal registration.
2. Value the holdings.
3. Collect all income and dividends owed.

4. Settle all transactions (buy-sell orders) initiated by the money managers.
5. Provide monthly reports that detail transactions, cash flows, securities held and their current value, and change in value of each security and the overall portfolio since the previous report.

Section V: Ethics Statement

This ethics statement shall apply to the Standards Director, service providers, and any other persons involved with the preparation, implementation, and maintenance of this PWPS.

Such persons **must**:

* Act in the best interest of the wealth holder and to the highest standards of professionalism.
* Maintain independence and objectivity in managing the wealth management strategy.
* Avoid all conflicts of interest, either real or perceived.
* Maintain the confidentiality of all information about the wealth holder.
* Acknowledge this ethics statement annually.

Such persons **may not**:

* Engage in any form of fraudulent or misleading conduct or commit any act that reflects adversely on their honesty, trustworthiness, or professional competence.
* Take any action that is contrary to the interests of the wealth holder.
* Take any financial interest (other than small amounts of stocks or bonds in publicly traded companies) in a company controlled by a service provider.
* Take any consulting, contract, or employment relationship with a service provider (outside the scope of this PWPS).
* Take receipt of any gifts, gratuities, or excessive entertainment from a service provider.

The Standards Director periodically will review compensation agreements, service agreements, and contracts of service providers to ensure that they do not contain provisions that:

1. Conflict with the wealth holder's goals and objectives
2. Include performance-based compensation formulas that are based on short- to intermediate-term (less than five years) investment results

Section VI: Persons Serving in a Fiduciary Capacity

Persons serving in an investment fiduciary capacity (trustee, investment committee member, investment consultant, or money manager) will comply with a fiduciary standard of care defined, at a minimum, by the following steps and dimensions:

Step 1: Analyze

1.1: State goals and objectives
1.2: Define roles and responsibilities of decision makers
1.3: Brief decision makers on objectives, standards, policies, and regulations

Step 2: Strategize (RATE)

2.1: Identify sources and levels of **R**isk
2.2: Identify **A**ssets
2.3: Identify **T**ime horizons
2.4: Identify **E**xpected outcomes (performance)

Step 3: Formalize

3.1: Define a strategy that is consistent with RATE
3.2: Ensure the strategy is consistent with implementation and monitoring constraints
3.3: Formalize the strategy in detail and communicate

Step 4: Implement

4.1: Define the process for selecting key personnel to implement the strategy

4.2: Define the process for selecting tools, methodologies, and budgets to implement the strategy

4.3: Ensure that service agreements and contracts do not contain provisions that conflict with objectives

Step 5: Monitor

5.1: Prepare periodic reports that compare performance with objectives

5.2: Prepare periodic reports that analyze costs, or return on investment, with performance and objectives

5.3: Conduct periodic examinations for conflicts of interest, self-dealing, and breaches of a code of conduct

5.4: Prepare periodic qualitative reviews or performance reviews of decision makers

Section VII: Inputs Used to Develop the Wealth Management Strategy

The Standards Director shall ensure that the wealth management strategy shall incorporate and reflect the following key inputs.

Time Horizon

The wealth management strategy is based on an investment horizon of greater than five years. Interim fluctuations should be viewed with appropriate perspective. Similarly, the PWPS's strategic asset allocation is based on this long-term perspective. Short-term liquidity requirements are anticipated to be met by a _____% allocation to cash.

Sources and Levels of Risk

The Standards Director recognizes the difficulty of achieving the PWPS's investment objectives in light of the uncertainties and complexities of contemporary investment markets. The Standards Director also recognizes some risk must be assumed to achieve the PWPS's long-term investment objectives.

Performance Expectations

The desired investment objective is a long-term rate of return on assets that is at least _____%, which is _____% greater than the anticipated rate of inflation. The target rate of return for the PWPS has been based on the assumption that future real returns will approximate the long-term rates of return experienced for each asset class.

The Standards Director realizes market performance varies and a _____% rate of return may not be meaningful during some periods. Accordingly, relative performance benchmarks for money managers are set forth in the Control Procedures section. Over a complete business cycle, the overall annualized total return, after deducting for advisory, investment management, and custodial fees, as well as total transaction costs, should perform favorably against a customized index comprised of market indices weighted by the PWPS's strategic asset allocation.

Asset Class Guidelines

The Standards Director believes long-term investment performance, in large part, is primarily a function of asset class mix. The Standards Director has reviewed the long-term performance characteristics of the broad asset classes, focusing on balancing the risks and rewards. The following asset classes were selected and ranked in ascending order of risk (least to most): [The following is provided only as an example.]

Money Market (MM)
Intermediate Bond (IB)
Large-Cap Value (LCV)
Large-Cap Blend (LCB)
Large-Cap Growth (LCG)
Mid-Cap Blend (MCB)
Small-Cap Blend (SCB)
International Equity (IE)

The Standards Director has considered the following asset classes for inclusion in the asset mix but has decided to exclude these asset classes at the present time: [The following is provided only as an example.]

Global Fixed Income
Real Estate

Rebalancing of Strategic Allocation

The percentage allocation to each asset class may vary as much as plus or minus _____% [suggest 5%], depending on market conditions. When necessary and/or available, cash inflows/outflows will be deployed in a manner consistent with the strategic asset allocation of the PWPS. If the Standards Director judges cash flows to be insufficient to bring the PWPS within the strategic allocation ranges, the Standards Director shall decide whether to effect transactions to bring the strategic allocation within the threshold ranges.

Section VIII: Money Manager and Custodian

At a minimum, the money manager due diligence process should include a review of the following: [The actual due diligence process will vary from country to country, depending on the availability of investment products and regulatory structure.]

1. The money manager has a defined investment strategy that is consistent with the wealth holder's goals and objectives and can be understood and explained to others by the wealth holder or the Standards Director.
2. The money manager has a defined investment strategy that can be monitored by the Standards Director.
3. The same investment management team has been in place for a period commensurate with the period of the performance evaluation.
4. Securities in the money manager's portfolio are consistent with the stated investment strategy.
5. Investment performance has been verified by an independent third party and compared to the money manager's peers.
6. Investment performance adjusted for risk has been compared to the money manager's peers.

7. The money manager's fees and expenses have been compared to the money manager's peers.
8. The investment structure (separate account, mutual fund, commingled trust, hedge fund) is appropriate for the given strategy and the Standards Director's ability to monitor the strategy.

At a minimum, the custodian due diligence process should include a review of the following: [The actual due diligence process will vary from country to country, depending on the availability of investment products and regulatory structure.]

1. As a best practice, custodians are independent of money managers, except as may be required by trust law or by the necessity of employing a commingled investment vehicle.
2. Custodian can provide appropriate security of assets, with insurance or otherwise.
3. Custodial statements provide sufficient detail that the Standards Director can monitor the money manager's best execution of trades (generation of soft dollars).
4. The expense ratio of the custodian's cash sweep and money market fund is compared to peers.
5. Custodian can provide investment performance reports and tax reporting.

Section IX: Monitoring Procedures

The Standards Director shall ensure that performance reports are periodically produced to demonstrate the continued effectiveness of the wealth management strategy.

Performance Objectives

The Standards Director acknowledges fluctuating rates of return characterize the securities markets, particularly during short-term time periods. Recognizing that short-term fluctuations may cause variations in performance, the Standards Director intends to evaluate money manager performance from a long-term perspective.

The Standards Director is aware that the ongoing review and analysis of money managers is just as important as the due diligence implemented during the manager selection process. The performance of money managers will be monitored on an ongoing basis, and it is at the Standards Director's discretion to take corrective action by replacing a manager if he or she deems it appropriate at any time.

On a timely basis, but not less than quarterly, the Standards Director will review whether each money manager continues to conform to the search criteria outlined in the previous section, specifically:

1. The manager's adherence to the PWPS's investment guidelines
2. Material changes in the money manager's organization, investment philosophy, and/or personnel
3. Any legal or other regulatory agency proceedings affecting the money manager

The Standards Director has determined performance objectives for each money manager. Performance will be evaluated in terms of an appropriate market index and the relevant peer group.

Watch List Procedures

A money manager may be placed on a Watch List, and a thorough review and analysis of the money manager may be conducted, when:

1. A money manager performs below median for its peer group over a one-, three-, and/or five-year cumulative period.
2. A money manager's three-year risk-adjusted return (Alpha and/or Sharpe ratio) falls below the peer group's median risk-adjusted return.
3. There is a change in personnel managing the account.
4. There is a significant decrease in the product's assets.
5. There is an indication that the money manager is deviating from the stated strategy.
6. There is an increase in the product's fees and expenses.
7. Any extraordinary event occurs that may interfere with the money manager's ability to fulfill its role in the future.

A money manager evaluation may include the following steps:

* A letter to the money manager asking for an analysis of underperformance
* An analysis of recent transactions, holdings, and account characteristics to determine the cause for underperformance or to check for a change in style
* A meeting with the money manager, which may be conducted on-site, to gain insight into organizational changes and any changes in strategy or discipline

The decision to retain or terminate a money manager cannot be made by a formula. It is the Standards Director's confidence in the money manager's ability to perform in the future that ultimately determines the retention of a money manager.

Measuring Costs

The Standards Director will review, at least annually, all costs associated with the management of the investment program, including:

1. Expense ratios or fees of each investment option against the appropriate peer group
2. Custody fees: the holding of the assets, collection of the income, and disbursement of payments
3. Whether separate account managers are demonstrating attention to best execution in trading securities

Section X: Review of the PWPS

The Standards Director will review this PWPS with the wealth holder at least annually to determine whether stated investment objectives are still relevant, and the continued feasibility of achieving the same. It is not expected that the PWPS will change frequently. In particular, short-term changes in the financial markets should not require adjustments to the PWPS.

Prepared: **Approved:**
Standards Director   Wealth Holder

Index

Accidental wealth holders, wealth for, 4, 5
Accountable skills, 204
Active investment strategies, 189
Advisor fees, 202–3
AIG, x, 30, 48, 55, 58, 106, 108
Amgen, 60
Analysis in ethos decision-making framework, 123, 124, 125, 126, 127, 128, 129, 130, 131, 133–43
Analytical skills, 155
Antitrust violations, 40
Appropriateness, 45, 70–73
Assessment procedures, 213–19
Asset allocation, 23, 43, 44, 49–50, 69, 149, 167, 198
Asset classes, 54, 154

Balance sheet analytics, 69, 73
Banking crisis of 2008, 55
Bear Stearns, x, 106
Berkshire Hathaway, 51, 68
Biophilia, 27–28, 31–32
Boardroom risk, 149
Bonds, 46
Bundling, 24
Business efficiency, 23–24

Campden, 28
Capitalization, 69–73
Cargill, 53
Carnegie, 39
Cash, diversification of, 54–55
Cash equivalents, 4
Charitable foundations, 41–42
Charitable grants, 37
Charitable lead trusts, 45–46, 50, 85, 86
China, private wealth and, 18, 19
Code of conduct, difference between code of ethics and, 206
Comfort, 27–33, 145
Communicative skills, 175
Compensation, 92

Competent skills, 140
Concierge services, 22, 92
Consulting fees, 203
Contract review, 192–93
Control as purpose of wealth, 5–6, 11
Core holdings, diversification out of, 51–52
Corporations, 83
Counterparty risk, 64
Courageous skills, 179
Creativity in wealth management, vii, 6–7
Currency jurisdictions, 54
Currency risk, strategic value of managing, 46
Custodial charges, 203
Custodians, diversification and, 55
Cutting edge investments, 61

Dead hand, 83
Death, disposition at, 88–90
Debt, defining, 70
Debt analysis, 71
Decisions, hierarchy of, 157
Decisive skills, 165
Deliberative skills, 138
Derivatives, 47, 68
Diligent skills, 201
Disciplined skills, 191
Distrust, comfort and, 29
Diversification, 43, 50–59
Dollar return, 45
Due diligence, 25, 43, 55, 57, 58, 63–66, 153, 177–78, 182–87

Education
    investment, 43, 66–68
    next generation, 99–102
Emotional intelligence, 120
Employee salaries, 202–3
Endowments, investment of, 44
Enron, 58
Entrepreneurialism, 67
Equality, defined, 89–90
Estate planning, 4, 86–90

Ethics, 121
Ethos
    context of, 121–22
    decision-making process as basis of, 113
    defined, 121, 129
Ethos decision-making framework, 121–32
    breakdown of the, 132
    decision-making dimensions in, 124
    step 1: analysis in, 123, 124, 125, 126, 127,
        128, 129, 130, 131, 133–43
    step 2: strategize in, 123, 124, 126, 128, 129,
        130, 145–62
    step 3: formalize in, 123, 126, 128, 129, 130,
        163–75
    step 4: implement in, 123, 124, 126, 128, 129,
        131, 177–94
    step 5: monitor in, 123, 124, 126, 128, 129,
        131, 195–211
Exemplary skills, 188

Fair-minded skills, 194
Family, make up of, 17–18
Family legacy and values, 95–97, 213
Family limited partnerships, 82
Family monolith, 18
Family name, 39–41
Family Office Exchange, 28
Family offices, 17, 21–25, 90–93, 104–5
Family wealth, 19–21
    dispositions at death and, 88–90
    philanthropy in, 39
Family wealth conferences, 29
Family wealth management, 17, 23, 25
Family wealth steward, 6, 14
Fear, comfort and, 29
FedEx, 105
Fees, sensitivity to, 153
Fidelity, 55
Fiduciary responsibility, 14
Financial risks, 150
Financial services industry, 29–30, 105–6
Ford Motor Company, 53, 105
Formalize in decision-making framework, 123,
    126, 128, 129, 130, 163–75
Foundations, 37, 83
Freedom
    as purpose of wealth, 5–6
    from wealth, 11–15
Functionality, 5–6, 29, 40–42, 100

GE, 77
Genuine skills, 208
Gold, 57
Golden Rule, 97
Goldman Sachs, 25
Governance, 75–93
    estate planning and, 86–90
    family office and, 90–93
    succession and, 76–80

tax structuring and, 80–82
    trusts and, 82–86
Goverance risk, 150
Growth investor, 60

Hazard risks, 150
Hedge funds, 13
Home Depot, 60
Hong Kong, philanthropy in, 38

IBM, 68
Implement in decision-making framework,
    123, 124, 126, 128, 129, 131, 177–94
Incapacity, 85
Incentive trusts, 84
Incidentals, use of wealth for, 7
India, wealth in, 19–20
Individuality, wealth and, 17–25
Industry weighting, 45
Innovative skills, 147
Institute for Private Investors, 28
Institute for Wealth Management Standards,
    xi, 108
Institutional wealth, goals of, 43–44
Institutional wealth management, ix
Integrity, 107
Intelligence, emotional, 120
Intelligent skills, 135
Intestacy, laws of, 88
Investment advisory work, elements in, 65
Investment education, 43, 66–68
Investment policies, 43–68
    asset allocation in, 43, 49–50
    diversification in, 43, 50–59
    investment education in, 43, 66–68
    investment styles in, 43, 59–63
    performance measurement in, 43, 45–46
    transparency in, 43, 47–48
    volatility in, 43, 47–48
Investments
    cutting edge, 61
    passive, 60–61, 68, 189
    socially responsible, 62–63
    styles of, 43, 59–63
    vanilla, 66
Investors, 60, 68

Johnson Wax, 53
Jurisdiction, diversification and, 56

Leadership, 118–20
Legacy wealth, time horizons for, 44
Lehman, x, 15, 30, 48, 55, 57, 58, 106,
    108
Liabilities, 69
Lifestyle, diversification and, 59
Limited liabilities companies, 83
Liquidity, diversification and, 57
Liquidity risk, 149

Lost opportunity risk, 149
Lowenhaupt Global Advisors' Global Council, xi, xiii, 106, 107, 108

Madoff, Bernie, x, 15, 30, 48, 61, 64, 91, 103, 106, 107, 108, 109, 133, 195
Managers, diversification and, 57–59
Micromanagement, 91
Microsoft, 19
Minnesota Mining, 60, 68
Money manager fees, 202–3
Money market funds, 54
Monitor in decision-making framework, 123, 124, 126, 128, 129, 131, 195–211
Monte Carlo simulation, 47, 49, 59
Morgan, J. P., 83, 109
Motivational skills, 211
Multigenerational wealth, 21, 39, 68
Mutual funds, 190–91

Next generation education, 99–102
Nikkei 225, 46

Opaqueness, 48
Operational risks, 150
Outsourcing, 58, 65
Ownership, 18–19, 68

Partnerships, 83
Passive investments, 60–61, 68, 189
Patient skills, 158
Per stirpes disbursement of wealth, 24
Performance analysis, time horizons in, 44
Performance attribution analysis, 199
Performance-based fees, 207
Performance expectations, 160, 161
Performance measurement, 43, 45–46, 199
Perpetuity, 83
Philanthropy, 7–8, 37–42, 86, 92, 100
Portfolio management, 30
Portfolios, strategic design of, 50
Pragmatic skills, 172
Preservation, 6–7, 51
Primogeniture, 19–20, 21
Principles of Wealth Management for Private Wealth Holders and Related Parties, xi, 106–9
Private wealth, ix–x
    in China, 18, 19
    goals of, 43–44
    management of, ix, x
Private wealth holders
    appropriateness for, 45
    principles of Wealth Management for, xiv–xv
    taxes for, 44
Private Wealth Policy Statement, 117, 164, 173–74, 221–34
Procedural skills, 143

Process, as foundation of sound wealth management, 103
Protection, 5–6
Prudent skills, 151
Purchasing power risk, 149
Pure quantitative analytics, 68
Purpose skills, 162

Refugee mentality, 59
Return, investment performance and, 45
Risk
    analysis of, 148
    connotations of, 148
    counterparty, 64
    defined, 149
    types of, 149, 150
Risk matrix, 149–50
Risk tolerance, 47, 59
Rockefeller, 39
Rothschild, 53

Schwab, 55
Securities framework, 30
Self-actualization, 5, 6, 11, 15
Seneca, 3
Servant leadership, 119
Sharpe, William, 167
Short-term obligations, 54
Situational leadership, 120
SMART, 160, 161
Social, relationship or entitlement risks, 150
Social entrepreneurship, 39
Socially responsible investments, 62–63
S&P 500 Index, 46
Standards Director, xi, 117–20
    accountable skills of, 204
    analytical skills of, 155
    communicative skills of, 175
    competent skills of, 140
    courageous skills of, 179
    decisive skills of, 165
    deliberative skills of, 138
    diligent skills of, 201
    disciplined skills of, 191
    exemplary skills of, 188
    expertise of, 153
    fair-minded skills of, 194
    genuine skills of, 208
    innovative skills of, 147
    intelligent skills of, 135
    leadership role of, 118–20
    motivational skills of, 211
    patient skills of, 158
    pragmatic skills of, 172
    procedural skills of, 143
    prudent skills of, 151
    purpose skills of, 162
    self-assessment instrument for, 216–19

steadfast skills of, 216
strategic skills of, 169
Stanford Financial, x, 103, 108, 133, 195
Steadfast skills, 216
Stewardship, 20
Strategic analysis, 65
Strategic philanthropy, 38–39
Strategic skills, 169
Strategic thinking, vii
Strategize in decision-making framework,
   123, 124, 126, 128, 129, 130, 145–62
Strategy, importance of, 33–35
   capitalization, 69–73
   family legacy and values, 95–97
   governance, 75–93
   investment policies, 43–68
   next generation education, 99–102
   philanthropy, 37–42
Succession, 76–80

Taxes
   governance and, 80–82
   wealth and, 4
Time horizons
   of investment portfolios, 156
   in performance analysis, 44
Trading costs, 203
Transactional leadership, 120
Transformational leadership, 120
Transparency, 43, 48–49
Transportation regulatory framework,
   30
Trustees
   in common law jurisdiction, 18
   selection of, 84
Trusts, 82–86, 107
Trustworthiness, 30

UBS, 82
Unbundling, 22

Value investor, 60
Vanilla investments, 66
Volatility, 43, 47–48

Wealth
   freedom from, 11–15
   in India, 19–20
   individuality and, 17–25
   multigenerational, 39, 68
   per stirpes disbursement of, 24

   preservation of, 6–7
   purpose of, 3–9, 11
   self-actualization and, 5, 6
   taxes and, 4
   use of, for incidentals, 7
   for the wealth inheritor, 12–13
Wealth conferences, 4
Wealth consumers, raising children as, 14–15
Wealth creation, 6–7, 43
Wealth creators, 18, 20–21
Wealth holders
   accidental, 4, 5
   decision making by, 31–32
   delegation of wealth management by, 15
   expertise of, 153
   need for strategy, 33
   purpose of wealth for, 3–9
Wealth industry, family wealth management
   and, 17
Wealth inheritor, wealth and, 7–8, 12–13
Wealth management, 12
   biophilia and, 28
   creativity in, ix
   effective, 35
   institutional, ix
   multigenerational, 21
   principles of, ix–xv
   private, ix, x
   qualitative factors that affect, 209
   strategic thinking in, ix
   strategy in, 33–35
   trustworthiness in, 30
   wisdom in, ix
Wealth management ethos, framework associated
   with, 112–14
Wealth management programs
   building, 8
   philanthropy in, 37–42
   utilizing elements of, for education, 102
Wealth management standards, role of, 103–9
Wealth preservation, 43
Wealth schools, sending children to, 99
Wealth steward, 6, 12, 14
Weavering, 30
Wisdom
   as foundation of sound wealth management,
      103
   getting, 6
Workout, 72

Xerox, 68

About the Authors

Charles A. Lowenhaupt is one of the world's most respected experts on wealth management for ultra-high-net-worth families. Lowenhaupt is the founder and chief executive officer of Lowenhaupt Global Advisors, LLC, which serves global families of significant wealth. He is also managing member of the affiliated law firm Lowenhaupt and Chasnoff, LLC, which was founded by his grandfather in 1908 as the first U.S. law firm to concentrate in income tax law.

Lowenhaupt is a founding advisory faculty member of the Institute for Private Investors, and he advises the Institute as an emeritus member of the advisory faculty and contributor to its programs. Until recently, he served with Don Trone as a director of the Foundation for Fiduciary Studies in Pittsburgh. With Trone, he founded the Institute of Wealth Management Standards and now serves as president of the Institute. Lowenhaupt has a bachelor of arts degree from Harvard University. He also has a juris doctorate from the University of Michigan Law School and is a member of the Order of the Coif. He is a member of the bar of New York and Missouri.

Lowenhaupt brings to this volume the experience of working with wealth holders and their families for more than 100 years. Six generations of families have worked with three generations of the Lowenhaupt family dating back to 1908. In addition, Lowenhaupt draws on his involvement and conversations with wealth holders and trusted advisors around the world. Insights from those conversations inform his views about wealth management and serve as a catalyst for much of what he writes and does professionally.

Donald B. Trone is the CEO (Chief Ethos Officer) of 3ethos, is the former director of the United States Coast Guard Academy Institute for Leadership, and is the founder of the Foundation for Fiduciary Studies.

Trone has been named by numerous organizations as "one of the most influential people" in the retirement, financial planning, and investment advisory industries. In 2003, he was appointed by the U.S. secretary of labor to represent the investment counseling industry on the ERISA Advisory Council, and in 2007, he testified before the Senate Finance Committee on fiduciary issues associated with retirement plans investing in hedge funds.

Trone graduated as president of his class from the United States Coast Guard Academy and served on active duty for ten years, including six years as a long-range search-and-rescue helicopter pilot. He received his master's degree in financial services from the American College and has completed postgraduate studies at Pittsburgh Theological Seminary and Trinity Episcopal Seminary.

Trone brings to this book the Ethos framework—the discipline, rigor, and process that binds principles to standards. His approach is drawn from spending the past 25 years developing standards and training programs for investment fiduciaries.